EDWARD BOUVERIE PUSEY

PUSEY

by

LEONARD PRESTIGE

with introduction by
Canon Cheslyn Jones

MOWBRAY
LONDON & OXFORD

Introduction © Cheslyn Jones, 1981

ISBN 0 264 66869 3

This edition published 1982 by
A. R. Mowbray & Co. Ltd., Saint Thomas House,
Becket Street, Oxford, OX1 1SJ

The text was first published 1933
by Philip Allan & Co. Ltd., and is reproduced
offset, from Simson & Co. Ltd.'s
original printing, by
The Thetford Press, England

CONTENTS

	Introduction by Canon Cheslyn Jones	*page* vii
	PREFACE	xv
I	LOVERS' MEETINGS	1
II	PROFESSOR PUSEY	17
III	THE OXFORD MOVEMENT	32
IV	PATERFAMILIAS	44
V	OUTCAST	61
VI	VIA CRUCIS	77
VII	THE TURN OF THE TIDE	95
VIII	A FATHER IN ISRAEL	113
IX	THE BRIDGE-BUILDER	129
X	THE REVOLT OF THE CATHOLIC LAITY	142
XI	JOURNEY'S END	160

INTRODUCTION

Refurbishment is the order of the day for Victorian houses; also, it seems, for the Victorian biographies of their ecclesiastics, including the leaders of the Oxford Movement. We already have Georgina Battiscombe's *John Keble* (1963); David Newsome has done wonders for the Wilberforce brothers and the early Manning in *The Parting of Friends* (1966); Piers Brendon's use of new material has produced *Hurrell Froude and the Oxford Movement* (1974). The appearance of *The Letters and Diaries of John Henry Newman*, edited by C. S. Dessain of the Birmingham Oratory, from 1961 onwards has added further raw material to an already flourishing industry. But in the case of Edward Bouverie Pusey, the tough spine of those who remained faithful to the Church of England, nothing comparable has yet happened; the chief printed source remains H. P. Liddon's massive biography, in four volumes, over two thousand pages in all. 16 September 1982 brings us to the centenary of Pusey's death, and those who celebrate the occasion will require at least an outline biography. It would be impossible to reprint Liddon's work as it stands; so we present a shorter biography by the late Dr G. L. Prestige, itself an acknowledged abbreviation of Liddon. We are grateful to his son and daughter for permission to reprint it.

Why, we may ask, has Dr Pusey failed to attract refurbishment? After all, he has many claims to our interest, over and above his scholarly and indestructible allegiance to the ecclesiastical title-deeds of the Anglican Church as an authentic part of the catholic church of

Christ. As the biography will show, he was, despite his inclinations, no cloistered academic; he was active in promoting the building of churches in industrial areas and in establishing the church in colonies overseas; he was a pioneer in the foundation of religious communities, and later in attempting 'ecumenical' dialogue with Rome. In addition, his social and academic upbringing and status gave him wider contacts in England than any other Tractarian figure, as is shown by his being related to Lord Shaftesbury and by his lifelong contact with Gladstone, consummated in the congregation of notables at his funeral.

There are two points in particular on which we in England are in Pusey's debt; both arise from his visits to Germany, briefly referred to on p. 13 and p. 18. Attention is often concentrated on his reaction to German theology, or on the fact that he laid aside his proficiency in oriental languages after he joined the Tractarians, probably because he found them of less use than he hoped for unravelling the Hebrew Old Testament. But the fact remains that fluency in German at that time was very rare among English scholars, and in that respect Pusey was among the pioneers. Further, he acquired the German habit of meticulous well-documented historical accuracy (often expressed in foot-notes), which became second nature to him, so that he found it impossible to work without rigorous reference to authorities. In other words he was one of the first to introduce German standards of historical scholarship into this country. His fellow countrymen have continued to apply these standards, even as he did, in criticism of German speculations or speculative conclusions. His scholastic standards were first felt in his contributions to the Tracts on Baptism. At the crisis provoked by the Gorham Judgment (pp. 87ff.), he allayed panic with 259 pages on the historical basis of the Royal Supremacy in relation to the Church. At the publication of *Essays and Reviews* (p. 105), again he did not panic, as he had met it all before in Germany.

We are also in his debt for his part in University Reform, at least in Oxford (pp. 96–100), owing to his thorough knowledge of German universities and their professors and students. Here he was not just a reactionary or an ecclesiastic; he had a genuine appreciation of educational methods and institutions. Being himself a professor very much in the German style, he saw clearly that the lecture of the omniscient professor is not a good instrument for the *first* degree, and vastly inferior to the contact of mind with mind as practised in the indigenous 'tutorial' system. His knowledge of German halls of residence for students enabled him to point out the benefits of the more structured community life available in the existing colleges. The survival, and indeed improvement, of the tutorial and collegiate systems in our ancient universities, two characteristics for which they are most valued, is largely due to Pusey's efforts.[1]

Perhaps the foremost deterrent against the refurbishment of Pusey is provided by these very factors, his many-sidedness, the extent of his contacts, the length of his life, as well as by the range of documentation which he shares with others of his age. In the Pusey Memorial Library alone, not to mention other collections, the sources would challenge, and might well defeat, any individual mastery.

Others may be deterred by Liddon's four massive volumes: what more could be added to them? Investigation of limited topics may not bear this out. Dr

---

1. On this see the Report and Evidence upon the recommendations of Her Majesty's Commissioners for inquiry into the state of the University of Oxford (1853); Pusey's evidence covers pp. 1–174.

David Forrester's article on *Dr Pusey's Marriage* (Ampleforth journal LXXVII (1973) pp. 33–47), researched very largely from sources left by Liddon, gives a very different impression from the official biography; as also does Dr H. G. C. Matthew's article on Pusey's theological evolution (Journal of Theological Studies, N.S. XXXII, April 1981, pp. 101–124). These are only two straws in the wind, suggesting that there is scope for much further research in preparation for a fresh reappraisal.

But, although it is seldom mentioned, there is no doubt that Pusey's penitential discipline has been the greatest deterrent. Liddon, who apparently exercised such reticence about Pusey's courtship and marriage, decided to print *in extenso* the penitential rule of life, which he came to adopt when a widower and which he submitted to Keble in connection with his first confession in 1846 (Liddon III, pp. 106–108; Prestige, pp. 51–53). Pusey is consequently judged as a morbid, introspective character, to be shunned as an unwholesome influence. Pusey has been doubly unlucky, in that spiritual attitudes have changed considerably in the course of this twentieth century; penitential rigour has now few apologists.

We must remember that his penitential habits were not imposed suddenly or after purely rational calculation; his instincts had been leading him in that direction from the time he became a widower seven years earlier, so that by 1846 these habits might well have become second nature to him. We must also remember that penitence was not the whole of his religion; it was balanced by other factors. Prestige asserts that 'Pusey was not morbid'; '. . . he walked with God . . .'; 'he had not retired into himself but into God' (pp. 53, 54). Prestige was right; but contemporary Christians will want more than Prestige's word for it. Only Pusey himself can reassure us; for that let him take us to a little-used source, his own published sermons.

Newman's sermons, particularly those of his Anglican days, are often studied; they were, and remain, one of his chief attractions. The late C. S. Dessain has pointed out that they broke new ground both with regard to the wide range of human feeling which they reflected and with regard to the full range of Christian doctrine which they covered, echoing the complete cycle of the liturgical year (*John Henry Newman*, 3rd edition, O.U.P. 1980, chapters 2 and 4). Both claims could be made equally well for Pusey's sermons; indeed one could go further to claim more human *pathos* and even deeper elaboration of doctrine. There is much to prick the conscience of the hardened sinner, of the recidivist or of the luxurious, as we would expect. But there is also much that expresses joy and hope, not to mention love, in their higher reaches, and the life of God himself which we are called to share. Like Newman, he stresses the reality of the divine indwelling in the soul. We will bring this introduction to a close with a few examples, which not only confirm Prestige's verdict but also place Pusey high on the list of mystics, of those with a genuine, first-hand experience of God.

> God is the Lord, the Father, the Centre of the soul. The soul must turn wholly to Him for its life, its light, its peace, its joy, its resting place, all good to it, all goodness in it. As the flower follows the sun, and opens itself to its glow, and through that glow sends forth its fragrance, and ripens its fruit, so the soul must turn to Him, the Sun of Righteousness, unfold itself wholly to His life-giving glow, hide nothing from his searching beams, and through the fire of his love ripen to Him the fruits of His Spirit. (*Parochial and Cathedral Sermons* (1882), p. 20).

Peace is not our end, my brethren, but holiness and the service of God, and the love of God, and union with God, of which peace is the fruit. Seek not peace then for itself; but seek God, seek Jesus Who is our Peace. If ye seek to find peace for yourselves, you may be deceived by a false peace. If you surrender your whole selves to God, if you give up to Him every desire out of Him, if you long to be, to have, all and only that, which God willeth you to be and to have; if with a whole heart you desire to be His, and that He should be your God, then you will have some earnest and foretaste of that heavenly joy. Then in the joy of that self-surrender, weak and faint though it be, you will have, in some degree, the witness of God that you are His, who has given you the desire to be His. (*ibid.* p. 182).

As here the body ministers to the soul, so also there, not only in these poor earthly pleasures, but as fitted to its new state of being; overstreamed with delights, but incapable of suffering; transported with love and united to those it loves, but itself too, spiritual; joying in beauty, but the beauty of God, the beauty of souls and bodies resplendent with God. The pure pleasures and joys of this poor body too shall be higher, purer, more spiritual, far, than the purest pleasures which the purest soul can conceive here. For soul and body shall be forever indwelt by God, transformed by God into a spiritual nature, which the heart of man cannot conceive now. (*ibid.* p. 413–4).

Leonard Prestige

George Leonard Prestige, who was born in 1889 and died as a Canon of St Paul's Cathedral in 1955, was one of the leading Christian scholars of his day. From Merchant Taylor's' School he gained a scholarship to Christ Church, Oxford, where he distinguished himself with three 'firsts' in classics and theology. He was ordained in 1913 on a fellowship at New College; after seven years he proceeded to the college living of Upper Heyford, in north Oxfordshire, where he performed the duties of a country incumbent from 1920 to 1944. Heyford was in easy reach by rail of both Oxford and London. In relation to Oxford, he worked for the *Lexicon of Patristic Greek*, then under the editorship of my predecessor, Dr Darwell Stone, and was assigned the major articles on the technical theological terms used in the elaboration of the doctrines of the Trinity and Incarnation. The *Lexicon* eventually appeared in 1961, and its final editor, Dr Geoffrey Lampe, has testified to the high and permanent quality of Prestige's earlier work. From this firsthand study of the Fathers' usage Prestige also culled the material for *God in Patristic Thought* (1936), one of the most original and creative books on historical theology of this century, which quickly established his name as a leading patristic expert. From the same quarry he planned a second book, on Christ in patristic thought, which eventually became the Bampton Lectures of 1940, delivered and published under the title *Fathers and Heretics* (colloquially known in the profession as Dads and Cads).

Prestige not only had a scholarly pen but also a talent for biographical writing; this book on Pusey was his first essay in this direction, though he is best known for his *Life of Charles Gore* (1935). This talent also extended to journalism, to London, and the staff of the *Church Times*, of which he was finally Editor from 1941 to 1947. After a brief period on the Church of England Council for Foreign Relations (during which he initiated the first informal theological discussions with Roman Catholics, which have since flowered into the Anglican–Roman Catholic International Commission), he became a Canon of St Paul's for his remaining years. There too his pen continued at work in compiling the history of the cathedral between

1831 and 1911, published after his death as *St Paul's in its Glory* (1955).

Prestige's *Pusey* was written for the centenary of the Oxford Movement, as one of a series on the Tractarian leaders. So it is nearly fifty years old, and may itself be thought to need a little refurbishment. Modern readers may never have seen a 'biretta' on or off a priest's head (p. 152) or a Church of England bishop, dean or archdeacon in buttoned gaiters, as if on horseback, with ariels on his hat (p. 111). As an ecclesiastical journalist Prestige spiced his narrative of the nineteenth century with sideglances at the enthusiasms of the Oxford Movement Centenary and the current Anglo–Catholic Congresses. On pp. 57, 76 and 156, for instance, there are references to bishops which hardly apply to their tamer, synodical, successors, phrased in tones of an antagonism which has largely been outlived. On p. 27 readers will need to know that the Deposited Book was the Alternative Service Book, rejected by Parliament in 1927 and 1928, most of which survives under the legalised and innocuous label of 'Series I'. And the Public Worship Regulation Act of 1874 has eventually been taken off the statute book (see p. 159). These details, of course, in no way affect the substance of the biography.

Pusey House
Oxford

CHESLYN JONES
1 November 1981

PREFACE
(*to original edition*)

MOST, THOUGH NOT ALL, of the facts of Dr. Pusey's life which possess abiding interest are contained or have reference made to them in the large four-volume *Life* prepared by Dr. Liddon; and they may be excavated from that work by diligent research. The present writer is indebted to the courteous permission of its publishers, Messrs. Longmans, Green & Company, for freedom to draw on the facts collected therein. For the inferences made, and the interpretations suggested, he alone is responsible.

G. L. P.

Chapter I

LOVERS' MEETING

"I HAVE THIS MORNING had the honour of receiving your Grace's letter informing me that His Majesty has been graciously pleased to approve of my being appointed to the Regius Professorship of Divinity in this University." In these terms one of the most brilliant in the group of young men who adorned the Oxford of 1828 began his acknowledgments to the Prime Minister, the Duke of Wellington, for a post which in strict fact he had not been offered. Shy, diffident, and romantical, Edward Pusey was apparently so overcome by the greatness of his good fortune that he was rendered incapable of transcribing correctly the title of the Regius Professorship of Hebrew, and proceeded to give thanks for what he had not received.

Yet there was good ground for emotional ecstasy, if not for the slight inaccuracy with which it was expressed. The appointment brought down the curtain on as fair a romantic comedy as could be witnessed on any historical stage. It set an early crown of fulfilment on an academic career which was already one of great distinction. It established Pusey in Oxford instead of, possibly, Bonn or some other 'pretty' German University town, with the idea of which he had been dallying. It afforded a competence for the support and a social position for the comfort and diversion of his newly-married wife; no happier consummation could have been devised for the fruition of love's young dream, so long postponed, so desperately mourned, and so unexpectedly fulfilled, as his had been. Last, and undoubtedly least, it solved a serious housing problem. In the lives of individuals the guidance and overruling of divine Providence, in things both great and small, often pursue a slow and apparently underground course over a long period, only to break at last into the open with a decisive action which reveals the whole purpose of the previous meandering. Such an event marks off an epoch. A section of the past is definitely closed, and a new prospect opens, to which all that has gone before is recognizably preparatory. In Pusey's life it is easy to observe the incidence of such providential divisions, but none is more emphatically marked than the wholly pleasant and gratifying occasion of his first and last ecclesiastical preferment. It confirmed the object to which the whole of his existence had been tending, and decided the tenor of his entire remaining life.

Edward Bouverie Pusey was the second son of the squire of Pusey, near Faringdon, in Berkshire, and of Lady Lucy, his wife. He was born on 22nd August 1800. His father was elderly, strongly Conservative, and rather exacting in his domestic and social discipline, but a man of great goodness and integrity, and able in spite of his formal ways to inspire affection as well as respect in his children. When he died his two elder sons described him on his memorial as 'pious and bounteous': both epithets were justified by abundant evidence. But it was to his mother that Pusey owed most of his early training, for which he never ceased, to the end of his long life, to express his thankfulness. Lady Lucy was a woman of strong character and regularly ordered life, devoted to her husband and children, conscientious and unaffected, a great lady of the old school, who thoroughly believed in the principle of employing economy of words and professions, and letting actions speak for themselves. "All that I know about religious truth," Pusey used to say, "I learnt at least in principle, from my dear mother." She taught him the Church Catechism, but she also taught him the still more valuable lesson of regulating his life by a sincere adherence to religious principle.

Little Edward proved an apt and serious pupil. His natural talents were enhanced by industry and attention. It is worth remarking that he quickly excelled his brother, Philip, the young squire, who was his senior by a year, both in riding and shooting. The keeper under whose instruction he acquired the latter art explained the fact by Edward's superior care. "He do take more pains about it." This was one of his most striking characteristics throughout life.

At the age of seven he was sent to a preparatory school to coach for Eton. Here the discipline, both moral and intellectual, was severe ; but it had the effect of laying good foundations for his future career, and he entered Eton at the beginning of 1812 with the habits formed of accurate scholarship and studious application. He formed but a few deep friendships at Eton. He was an intensely affectionate boy, but extremely shy. He rode well, and was a good swimmer, but his health was not robust, and he did not enter greatly into normal schoolboy games. He was happy in a manner, but it may be conjectured that his sensitive nature was somewhat repelled by the lack of privacy inseparable from the communal existence of a public school. His religious life does not appear to have been affected directly by his school experience, though he came to be recognized as a natural guide and philosopher to younger and less steady boys. The strongest impressions made on his reflective mind during this period of his life seem to have been occasioned by events of current politics, in which he continued to take an abiding interest, and in particular by the swift and dreadful judgment which fell on Bonaparte, the bogey of the early nineteenth century.

Young Edward had intended, for longer than he could himself remember, to take Holy Orders. He had settled on that vocation at least from the age of nine, and had no notion how the purpose arose. No other profession ever occurred to his mind. But soon after his leaving school, a second influence took hold of him which came to exercise scarcely less force on his mind and life than his choice of a career. He fell in love. It was the second grand passion of his life, and, like the first, it was a permanent devotion.

Pusey was now almost eighteen, and coaching with a tutor for Oxford. His parents were in the habit of exchanging yearly visits with a family named Barker, who lived fifteen miles away at Fairford. Pusey came home from his tutor's in the summer of 1818, to find such a visit in progress. It was thus at his own home that he first met Maria Barker, and was immediately attracted. Pusey was too shy to recognize the true nature of his own feelings towards her; his elder brother was the first to estimate them correctly. But the effect was profound. He had acquired a new and engrossing interest in life, second only to his passion for religious duty.

Nothing more passed between them at the time, but Maria henceforth shared with God the inner courts of his heart. She was just seventeen, gay, impulsive and accomplished. Ten years later she preserved a lightness of heart and, to judge from her portrait, an attractiveness of appearance which did more to conceal than to advertise an inner seriousness fit to match that of Pusey himself. When he first

5

met her, she must have seemed a wild and wholly delightful quarry; he alternately hoped for and despaired of her capture in his self-depreciating net. Pusey was the possessor of that sanguine temperament which leaps from the extreme of optimism to the corresponding depths of misery and gloom. Even from its early days, his love affair caused him exquisite depressions.

In January 1919 the young lover went up to Christ Church, but his thoughts were deeply occupied with Fairford. He worked steadily, and took an undergraduate interest in politics on the Liberal side, as young men of generous outlook are apt to do at that stage in their development. His elder brother became engaged to a lady of Whig family. The event appealed to Edward's politics; it spoke even more nearly to his heart. He hunted several times a week—always if the meet was in the direction of Fairford. When he was not hunting, he rode over the hills by which Oxford is surrounded, but by preference not to Shotover on the east, but to Foxcombe on the south-west—a lover's eye could almost persuade itself that from the top of Foxcombe it could see Fairford. He did not know that his affection was returned; but he could not endure to be parted from its object without leaving Maria some token of his passion. So he sent her a ring, anonymously addressing it to her through her father, without saying whence it came. Long afterwards he was desperately ashamed of this presumption, and could not remember whether he had disguised his handwriting or had got a friend to write the address. Perhaps it was fortunate for him that he committed himself thus, for Maria was attractive, and at one time cherished a certain enthusiasm for the Navy, which may not have been unconnected with some particular ornament of that service. At any rate, whether the origin of the packet was well disguised or ill, Maria guessed its source, and was grateful. Nor grateful only, but constant.

In the Long Vacation of 1821 Edward joined his brother Philip for a holiday in Paris. From the enjoyments of this trip he was recalled home to be informed that his parents had discovered the serious character of his attachment—which had apparently escaped them for two years after it was apparent to Edward's brother and to his friend Jelf—and that they disapproved of it. The original opposition apparently came from the other side. Mr. Barker had other views for his daughter's future, and refused to sanction any engagement with Pusey. Pusey's own father regarded the whole affair as a youthful infatuation for which time would afford a complete cure, and forbade his son to meet Maria. Edward was wholly dependent on his father; at least, until such time as he might hope to be ordained and presented to a living. He was also a dutiful as well as an affectionate son. His whole tradition constrained him to regard his father's word on such a matter as law. He obeyed without question.

But it almost broke him. He meditated leaving Oxford. He entertained some fears that he would go mad. His intermittent depression became a constant melancholy. For six years he never smiled, except occasionally when he forgot himself, an accident which was promptly corrected. It seems clear that Pusey was to some extent his own worst friend. Jelf, who had been his confidant all along, wrote him sensible and sympathetic letters. They may well have saved Pusey from the mental breakdown which he feared for himself and his conduct was calculated to encourage. At least they persuaded him to go on working for his degree and to trust in God. To make him hopeful or even cheerful was beyond their power.

He gave up riding, took no exercise, and tried to kill the pain of his emotions by hard work. He read the classics exhaustively, both those books which were required for his examinations, and those books which were not. It was even said that he worked for sixteen or seventeen hours a day. Fortunately, there was less than a year to run until he was in the schools, and, in spite of violent headaches, his health lasted, and he took a first class. One of his examiners said that Pusey was the man of the greatest ability that he had ever examined or known. Another, one no less brilliantly distinguished than John Keble, himself a poet, stated that he had never known how Pindar might be Englished until he heard Pusey construe him in the course of the examination. This is very odd, because later on in his life, though Pusey was a monument of industry, he cared nothing for style. But Keble's home was at Fairford, and the fact of having him for an examiner must on this occasion have struck genuine poetic fire from Pusey's flinty griefs.

It was now the summer of 1822. Pusey departed with a friend to Switzerland, where he admired the scenery, committed to writing, but in prose, the suggestions which it formed in his bosom, and drew parallels between the mountains and his own experiences. The fading of the after-glow on Mont Blanc reminded him of his private sorrows; the Jungfrau excited reflections on human character; sunrise over the Rigi inspired a comment on the superiority of revelation to natural religion. It was all very boyish, but it shows what subjects filled the boy's heart and mind. He triumphed with William Tell in the achievement of his country's emancipation from tyranny; but a more tender interest took possession of him when he beheld the Castle of Chillon. His soul was given over to what he afterwards came to call 'Byronism.' Byron was the recognized prophet of disappointed love, and the romantic spell of his literary pessimism lay heavy on Pusey, who, though he had declared that he "never arose from

reading Lord Byron a better man," was yet fasci-
nated by his pose of having emptied life's cup to the
dregs and found only disillusionment at the bottom.
Far as such an attitude was from representing the
judgment of Pusey's head, it expressed only too well
the misery of his feelings.

He returned after three months' indulgence in
romantic gloom to attend his brother Philip's
wedding to Lady Emily Herbert. This event was
an unmixed blessing to Edward. Lady Emily was a
warm-hearted person of considerable accomplish-
ments and great practical ability. She wrote a three-
volume novel in which Edward was figured with
photographic detail. What was of infinitely greater
importance, however, was that she formed a strong
attachment for her brother-in-law, entered warmly
into all his cares and anxieties, and provided him,
within the privileged circle of his own family, with
an intimate and understanding sympathy which
lasted undiminished to the end of her life. Her
friendship and affection both now and at later
crises afforded him a providential support and
consolation.

Meantime he plunged into fresh academic labours.
Certain friends had fallen into agnosticism. Pusey
was deeply shocked, and tried, not in every case
with great success, to restore their faith by argument. For this purpose he read the books which had
influenced them, with horror and shrinking. The

practical outcome for himself was that he decided not to assume parochial responsibilities when he should be ordained, but to devote his life to apologetic work, particularly on the Old Testament, which he saw was likely to bear the brunt of infidel attack. Even before taking his degree he had formed the intention of standing for a fellowship at Oriel. An Oriel fellowship was the chief prize of academic distinction in Oxford at the time, and was awarded by examination. His friend Jelf had secured one in 1821. But stronger than ambition, stronger even than his friendship for Jelf, was the desire to know John Keble, whose character inspired reverence and love far beyond his intimate acquaintance—and who spent his vacations with his father at Fairford. So Pusey, struggling with almost continuous ill-health, the reward of having driven tired nature too hard, worked through the winter at his books. The examination opened at the end of March 1823. On the first day Pusey had one of his severe headaches, tore up the essay which he had written, and threw it away. On the second day he wrote a letter asking leave to retire from the examination. But at last the fates were on Pusey's side. One of the Fellows picked up the pieces of the essay, which proved after a process of reconstruction to possess more merit in the eyes of the examiners than it had in those of its author. The answer to his note was an embassage desiring him to persevere. He went back to the hall, completed the examination, and at the end of the week was elected a member of the most brilliant and exclusive intellectual society of his day.

Keble left Oxford a few months later, but his influence on Pusey was immense. 'I always loved J.K. for his connection with Fairford,' wrote Pusey, 'but all he has said and done and written makes me esteem him more. There is a moral elevation in his character which I know in no other.' Another colleague was John Henry Newman, who had lodgings in the same house with Pusey, and went for walks with him, during which they talked religion, and Newman's self-confidence was somewhat abased by his companion's gentleness and humility. Thus in these first few months were laid the foundations of two friendships which were to prove of supreme importance in the course of Pusey's own life and in the history of the Church, friendships of an infinite fragrance and delicacy, and more durable even than life itself.

In addition to combating the infidelity of school friends, Pusey spent his time in studying theology under the guidance of Dr. Lloyd, the Regius Professor of Divinity, an old-fashioned but exceptionally thorough scholar. Little as Pusey realized the fact, the tide of his affairs had now decidedly turned. He had acquired strong and permanent interests, both practical and academic, in the study of theology; he had made friends of the two men out of the entire range of nineteenth century personalities whose character and attainments made their friendship most worth having to a man of religious sincerity and principle; and he had secured in Dr. Lloyd a patron whose intervention was decisive at the one moment of his life at which patronage was of importance to his private fortunes.

Though he was now of an age to be ordained, his occupations caused him to postpone ordination. In June 1824 the bells of Pusey parish church were rung to celebrate his winning of the University prize for a Latin essay on the Greek and Roman colonies. Another year passed in wrestling with theology and infidelity, and then on Dr. Lloyd's advice he paid a visit to Germany to learn the language and to study at first hand the critical and rationalist theories in vogue at German universities. He had by now finally determined to follow an academic, not a parochial, career. Much as he regretted the postponement of his ordination, it was clear that he must continue to learn before he could settle down to teach. In 1826 Dr. Lloyd sent him on a more prolonged sojourn in Germany, and in preparation for his projected life's work in defence of the Old Testament, he applied himself with dogged determination to the Oriental languages which bear on Hebrew research, working, as usual, incredibly hard, but forming useful acquaintances in academic circles, and purchasing folios of the ancient Church Fathers for Newman. When he returned to Oxford, after a year's absence, it was as one of the foremost young Orientalists in Europe.

In the interval Pusey's own family had dropped a hint that their objection to his engagement to Miss Barker was not irrevocable; but he did not take it seriously. The death of Mr. Barker put a somewhat different face on the affair. Mrs. Barker was encouraging to his suit. Edward and Maria met in September 1827 at Cheltenham, where Mrs. Barker was staying, and after nine bleak years, swooned deliriously but decorously into one another's arms. It was to him as 'the melting of the ice after a northern winter.' The frost thawed gradually. His first letters to her were rather of the nature of theological treatises. But Maria had sense, as well as overflowing humour; profound respect for her lover's learning and principles did not require her to smother the common transports of their mundane natures under a mattress of orthodox divinity. He found in her 'the attentive kindness which would not let me be grave, or which shared my gravity when it was overpowering.' In spite of the fact that he wrote his love-letters like lecture notes, and actually provided her with a key to the abbreviations most commonly employed in his script—he signed himself 'Your Edw.'—she taught him bit by bit to laugh and joke and play, and bullied him about epistolary 'stuffiness.' Slowly and tentatively the wilted Edward responded and began to lift up his head.

But the penalty of excessive strain and overwork had to be paid. He was compelled to spend the winter at Brighton under medical attention. His father then undertook to make him an allowance, so that his marriage need not be indefinitely delayed by the necessity of securing a professional income. The wedding was fixed for April 1828. Four days previously his father died suddenly, and it had to be postponed. Edward's spirits were thrown back into something of their old depression, but now that he had solid hopes to support him, the unhappiness of his father's loss was the better tempered with religious consolation. Dr. Lloyd had been appointed Bishop of Oxford, without relinquishing his professorship, while Pusey was in Germany. Pusey now returned to Oxford, read quietly, and was ordained deacon at Christ Church on 1st June by Dr. Lloyd. On 12th June, Edward and Maria were married in London by Jelf.

For three months they toured the Lakes and the Highlands, spending two days on their return with Sir Walter Scott at Abbotsford. The problem of a home and a career was in abeyance. They had no house, and the Oriel Fellowship ended with its holder's marriage. Bishop Lloyd lived at Cuddesdon in the episcopal residence. As the house pertaining to his professorship at Christ Church was vacant, excepting one room reserved for his books and his pupils, he invited the Puseys to occupy it temporarily, which they were very glad to do. At this point the Regius Professor of Hebrew died. Lloyd bestirred himself to secure the post for his brilliant and learned disciple. On 12th November the young people ended their stay as his guests, and retired to the ancestral home at Pusey, half inclined if nothing better turned up to settle among some of Edward's foreign friends at a German University. On 14th November the Duke of Wellington's letter arrived. Edward was to be the new Professor of Hebrew.

Nothing could have happened more opportunely. At one blow the Puseys secured a home, an occupation, an income, a position, a vocation; and all of the most agreeable kind. Their marriage was ideally happy; it was now to be established in an ideal setting. As Pusey could not, while he remained a deacon, be installed to the Canonry which accompanied the Professorship, Bishop Lloyd ordained him priest at Cuddesdon Parish Church on 23rd November. Christmas was spent at Pusey, where in the village church he celebrated the Holy Communion for the first time on the feast of the Nativity. His dearest hopes had all come to be realized in a few brief months. The winter was indeed past, and the miracle of spring had overtaken him with its fairest blossoms.

Chapter II

PROFESSOR PUSEY

MARRIAGE MADE NO DIFFERENCE to Edward Pusey's ingrained habit of industry. He took his wife round Oxford and showed her the sights. They entertained their numerous academic friends at little dinner parties. She paid a great number of calls; it is not clear, and may indeed be doubted, whether he always accompanied her. They knew everybody there was to know in Oxford, and had a carriage and pair with which to visit their friends outside it. The Canon's lodgings in the corner of Tom Quad at Christ Church became a busy social centre. But the real business of life went on without intermission or serious interruption; all the social activity was subsidiary to the life of study on which Pusey, and to some extent his wife, were engaged. Maria divided her literary enthusiasm between Latin historians, whom she could read with facility in the original, Whately's logic, and the British Navy; while her religious interest expended itself on the journal of Reginald Heber—the Missionary Bishop of India, and author of *Holy, Holy, Holy*, and *From Greenland's Icy Mountains*—together with some pretty stiff English theology and some German sermons. A young matron who was capable of all this intellectual vigour must be discharged from any imputation of being a mere butterfly. She earned her relaxations.

But Maria's glow of industry pales before the fire of Edward's literary occupations. Just before his engagement he had embarked single-handed, with Dr. Lloyd's connivance and encouragement, on a revised translation of the whole of the Old Testament. Though his health had broken down, his labours proceeded almost unchecked. Pusey was never the man to stop working merely because he was ill. But the plan was laid aside, through pressure of other commitments. Early in 1828 his interest in German theology, and the publication of an attack on it by Mr. Rose, a Cambridge theologian, led him to undertake an essay on the same subject. This work appeared in May. Pusey's innate optimism, of which his periodic depression merely represented the recoil that accompanies every forcible discharge of energy, caused him to estimate the tendencies of German theology more favourably than subsequent events and his own more mature judgment could justify. He recognized its 'rationalism,' which he ascribed to the stiffness and deadness of Lutheran traditionalism, but he was greatly impressed by the moral earnestness of some of the leaders, and hoped for a revival of the religious spirit, quickened by contact with scientific thought, but not dissipated by purely intellectual speculation. He was disappointed in his immediate expectations, and later repudiated the argument of his book.

To this day, German Protestant theology appears to be divided between two schools, of which the one tends to replace Christianity with speculative theological novelties, and the other to exalt religious interests by denouncing the application of any rational thought to the problem of their explanation. But Pusey's main concern was not with foreign difficulties. Though he was too modest to say so, his real object was to illustrate the dangers latent in the religious situation at home in England, where similar principles might be expected to lead to similar results. The old-fashioned High Churchmen, who owned a sincere respect for theology, were fanatically suspicious of religious emotion, which they designated 'enthusiasm,' and regarded as but little removed from demoniacal possession; the Evangelicals, who had done so much to revive and extend a practising religious spirit, were obsessed with a no less active dislike of theological knowledge. Pusey wished to combine the positive characteristics of both schools. He loved the Evangelicals 'because they loved our Lord; I loved them for their zeal for souls.' At the same time he was by nature, profession, and conviction, a theologian, and in a measure, a Liberal theologian; he knew that religion without an intellectual backbone was unstable and impermanent as a ripe cucumber. The *Theology of*

Germany was intended as a commentary for the Church of England.

Its publication had been followed by his ordination, marriage and professorship. At once his main activities were mortgaged to a new task. A second part of his criticism of German theology occupied him for a part of 1829, and issued from the press, after a good deal of private discussion, in 1830. But his chief work from the end of 1828 onwards was to complete the catalogue of Arabic manuscripts in the Bodleian Library, a task inherited from his predecessor in the Chair of Hebrew. An immense amount of work was necessary to bring this labour to a conclusion, as some of the manuscripts were mutilated, many of them were forgeries, and much of the preliminary work, which had been undertaken half a century before, had been very carelessly and inaccurately carried out. Pusey hated the drudgery that had to be expended on a task which effectually kept him from theology, the subject in which his heart lay. But for five years practically all his time was devoted to accomplishing this vast labour, and it was not until 1835 that he was finally quit of it. When at last he was free, he deserted Arabic with unconcealed relief, and sold all the books which he had amassed about that subject. He never intended to use them again, and had a good use for the money which was locked up in their possession.

In addition to his home and his work, a third great object of Pusey's interest and attention, which exercised in return a profound influence on his own life, lay in his friendships. He was on easy terms with both University and County. But he was far too busy, and, moreover, too shy and serious-minded, to have much time at his disposal for social gaieties outside Oxford. And inside the University his social relations were further restricted by the peculiarities of his position. A Canon of Christ Church and Regius Professor was a somewhat awful personage, below the sacred eminence which was still preserved for Heads of Houses, who confined their intimacies chiefly within the orbit of their own caste; but quite definitely superior to the ordinary Fellow of a college. Pusey was thus too great a man, academically considered, for ordinary residents to aspire to close familiarity with him, and too occupied to take great strides on his own part towards extending his intimacy much beyond the circle of his old colleagues and existing friends. He had many acquaintances, but few intimates. Of those to whom, beyond all other men, he gave the love and devotion of his whole nature without reserve, there were two, 'dear J.K.' and 'dear J.H.N.'

Pusey loved Keble and Newman with a wonderful and uncommon affection. As was only natural in the case of one whose life was founded on religion, his friendships were religious friendships. He had been originally attracted to Keble not only by the sentimental bond of common interests in Fairford, but still more by the virile sweetness of his character, the unassuming sincerity of his piety, and the disinterested grace and charm of his personality. Keble was eight years older than Pusey, and in many ways a contrast to the younger man. He was a Tory, while Pusey was a Liberal. He was retiring and was—wrongly—thought unpractical, while Pusey was always prominently active in the promotion of good works and right causes. He was a definite High Churchman, nurtured on the Caroline divines, long before Pusey thought of turning his attention in the direction of their writings. But he was a consecrated being; gentle as he was firm; playful and genial as he was austere; with an intellect as brilliant as his humility was 'humbling.' 'The cooling shadow of his lowliness' fell on Pusey as a breath from Paradise.

Keble retired from regular residence in Oxford in 1823, but visited the university at intervals, retaining his fellowship at Oriel till his marriage in 1835, and holding the Chair of Poetry from 1831 to 1841. It was not until 1835 that he accepted the Vicarage of Hursley, near Winchester, and up to that time he was still close at hand for purposes of consultation. At the end of 1827 he might have been elected Provost of Oriel. Pusey and Newman were among those who favoured the other candidate—"if we were electing an angel, I should of course vote for

Keble; but the case is different," observed Newman
—and Keble withdrew rather than provoke a con-
tested election. Pusey reproached himself to the very
end of his life on account of his own part in this
misjudgment of Keble's character and abilities. But
in 1829 Bishop Lloyd died, and the loss of this leader
and patron threw Pusey more into dependence on
his younger friends. The *Christian Year*, published
anonymously by Keble in 1827 at the request of his
father, was a book, as its author was a man, after
Pusey's own heart. Gradually, Pusey came to lean
more and more on Keble. By 1837 'dear J.K.' had
come to be recognized expressly by Pusey as his own
and Newman's 'father in the faith.'

Pusey's love for Newman was no less than that for
Keble, but differed from it, as the men differed on
whom the love was bestowed. Keble was the saintliest flower of the old High Church tree. Newman
was the austerest product of Evangelical enthusiasm,
and as such was suspect to J.K. The old High
Church School believed in murmuring the truth
rather than in proclaiming it. They had an exaggerated horror of publicity, and conscientiously
suppressed everything that might nowadays be
called the journalistic instinct. Orthodox theological
principles must be left to speak for themselves without advertisement; truth is great, and in the long
run prevails. Newman, both from nature and from
upbringing, held a different conception. He had all

the orator's desire to produce an effect, and all the Evangelical's passion to make public profession of his faith. He was constrained to testify and make disciples. He was incapable of leaving everything to God. His thought had been tempered by the orthodox but arid Liberalism of the logical school of Whately; but his heart remained Evangelical. Yet this quality endeared him to Pusey, in whose eyes 'dear J.H.N.' represented the living embodiment of proper Evangelical aggressiveness, just as 'dear J.K.' embodied the ideal of zealous practical theology. A synthesis of Pusey's two dear friends would have provided exactly a concrete illustration of the vision which he had in writing the *Theology of Germany*.

Pusey and Newman were therefore to be found perpetually conjoined in every conspiracy of good works. They were the two outstanding leaders of the younger Oxford generation. For Newman, too, like Pusey, had obtained a position, or at least, what was of greater importance to him, a platform. In 1828 he was appointed Vicar of St. Mary's, the University Church, and the long series of Sunday afternoon sermons began, which were to form the most impressive and influential moral witness to Christianity during the nineteenth century. A band of enthusiastic young disciples immediately gathered round him. But their leader was no longer a Liberal (as the name was then understood) in his theology. Before they came under Newman's leadership, some of the ablest of his disciples had already received the lasting imprint of Keble's mind. It was the providential mission of these disciples to teach their impressionable, and theologically unformed, master. Through their agency 'dear J.H.N.' became the disciple of 'dear J.K.'

The Newmanites were also friends of Pusey, but his intimacy was reserved for Newman in person. Pusey was not a member of the Newmanite group. So far as he followed anybody he followed Keble. But as Newman came more and more under Keble's influence, particularly after Hurrell Froude had succeeded in bringing Keble and Newman into personal association, the common link that they had with Keble formed an added bond between the Vicar of St. Mary's and the Professor of Hebrew. Two facts stand out concerning the origins of the Tractarian movement, the importance of which can hardly be exaggerated. The movement was the outcome of intimate personal friendships. And its theological basis was acceptance of the principles of John Keble. In that sense, Keble, the simple and silent, the strong and straightforward, was 'the true and primary author of the movement.'

Chief among the galaxy that revolved about the Vicar of St. Mary's, and the man who actually brought him into subjection to the theological discipline of Keble, was Hurrell Froude, who became a fellow of Oriel in 1826. Froude, who had been Keble's pupil, had imbibed his teaching with the devotion of a strongly original and independent conviction. Full of high spirits, and with an utter contempt for complacency and sham, Froude outraged the conventions of friend and foe with epigram and paradox. He and Newman struck sparks from one another's minds. Newman had the advantage in intellectual subtlety, Froude in the possession of a vigorous common·sense. Newman had the wider grasp, but Froude's prophetic humour, in spite of his horrifying sallies against accepted opinion, maintained a closer grip of practical realities. Moreover, Froude knew his own mind. Newman was always in danger from the receipt of new impressions. Novelty to him was apt to prove less illustrative than subversive of his convictions. But so long as Froude lived, he held Newman to his moorings with a cable of which the strands were challenge and inspired mockery, but at the end of which was an anchor of solid critical sense, fluked with insight.

The history of Pusey's theological development follows independent lines. He was educated under orthodox rather than High Church influence; which meant that he inherited no complete system of theology, but accepted the Bible and the Prayer Book, and thought for himself. The religion which he learned at his mother's knee was simple Prayer Book Christianity. In Pusey's early days it had not yet come to be reckoned a sign of disloyalty or party spirit to suppose that the Prayer Book means exactly what it says, nor had its plain sense been befogged by the invention of any Deposited Book, to make the Church unsafe for Anglicans. Consequently, he believed sincerely in priesthood and sacramental grace, and interpreted his Bible with the help of the Creeds provided for the purpose. The Bible was the foundation of his whole faith. It was, he wrote in 1823, the one book that was 'never to be out of our hands'; and the most fruitful, though of course for a religious teacher not the only necessary method of understanding its meaning was to compare it with itself. All that was needful for a learner was willing study with a teachable heart; a teacher required commentaries, of which it is significant that Pusey already recommends an ancient patristic commentary as the best. He assumes that the devout Churchman will read his Bible daily.

Though he loved the Evangelicals, he was fully prepared to chasten them with criticism, deprecating their insistence on the fewness of those who shall be saved, and objecting vigorously to their habit of judging religion by emotional intensity. "A *deep* repentance," as he justly observed, "is perfectly distinct from a *painful* or distressing one." But he was far more severe, at this early period, upon the Roman Catholics. As a political Liberal, he was keenly interested in the success of the agitation for Roman Catholic emancipation. But he strongly disliked the crucifixes which he saw in France in 1821. He is revolted by the 'abject and mercenary superstition' of the peasants in the Rhone Valley in 1822. And five years later the description which he sent Maria of St. Catharine of Siena imputes to the saint fanaticism and self-deceit as a certainty, with the possible addition of fraud. His sympathies were at this time far removed from any appreciation of Latin mysticism. He observed the fast days, because they were ordered in the Prayer Book, but without approving of the practice of austerities. And, though he regarded episcopacy as a blessing, he does not seem in 1830 to have realized as yet that it is so integral and organic a feature of the Christian Church that its absence from the Lutheran system might be expected to result in the existence of spiritual disorders.

In view of the sweeping change of attitude which came over his disciples of the third generation some sixty years later, on the subject of Biblical criticism, it is worth while remarking exactly the extent of Pusey's early liberalism, particularly as it was so far pronounced as to endanger for a time his prospects of being appointed to the Hebrew professorship. He drew a clear distinction between a theory of verbal inspiration, which extended Scriptural infallibility to the literal accuracy of every syllable and mark of punctuation in the sacred text; and a theory of religious inspiration, which merely guaranteed the religious truth expressed in Scripture without tying itself to such historical minutiæ as whether one or two blind men were healed on a given occasion. He expressly repudiated the former theory, and claimed in support of his general principles of inspiration the authority of Luther and numerous more modern divines, together with the ancient Fathers.

Obviously Pusey had not fully thought out his position. Nor did his view really coincide with the teaching of the Fathers, except in so far as it led him, like them, to value Scripture as a guide to religious doctrine and practice rather than as a depository of purely literary or antiquarian records. The time was not then ripe for revelation and historical criticism to make terms and kiss each other. The work of Samuel Driver, William Sanday, and Charles Gore was still below the horizon of the dawn. Pusey soon found himself forced to choose between desertion of the Liberal camp, for some of whose inmates both he and Newman had a deep regard, and abandonment of revelation to rationalist wolves. He chose the former alternative, withdrew his books on German theology from circulation, and forbade them to be reissued. Henceforward he was done with Biblical criticism of the modern type. But his youthful experiment possesses extraordinary interest, not simply as evidence of his own liberalism, in theology as in politics, but as forecasting the lines along which later advances were destined to be made.

He was emphatic that the special purpose of Scripture was to teach strictly spiritual truth. This object was not, in his view, to be secured by attributing to the Bible a mechanical infallibility. It is quite clear from his letter to Bishop Lloyd in 1828 that he regarded inspiration as operating on the mind of the Scriptural author rather than on the text of the sacred Book. It was the writers, not their writings, that were primarily inspired, and the primary effects of inspiration upon them were an understanding of religious truth and guidance in selection of those facts which were of importance for its transmission. Moreover, though he recognized the importance of maintaining that our Lord's discourses had been accurately preserved, he was quite definite in asserting that revelation was progressive. Our Lord's teaching was only a part of the material of revelation, and 'was not the main object of His coming into the world.' Christ was the object of revelation, not its chief agent. Neither our Lord's teaching, nor His acts, nor His person were fully understood at first. But taken all together, they constituted a body of material from which the full truth of the Christian religion could be inferred by the subsequent reflection of the Church, sharpened and guided by the inspiration of the Holy Ghost. Quite certainly Pusey, in opposing rationalism, was not afraid of recognizing the agency of human reason in deducing spiritual truth. 'Where doubts have acquired a general prevalence,' he wrote, 'it is an unquestionable service to collect these doubts as strongly as they are capable of being put.' Keble demurred. Learned doubts were unsettling to good simple folk. But Pusey rested his contention on the perfectly sound Liberal view that facts must be explained and not ignored, if truth in the long run is to prevail.

Chapter III

THE OXFORD MOVEMENT

PUSEY WAS STILL DEFINITELY a Liberal when the Reform Bill passed in 1832. The first Reformed Parliament was to meet early in 1833, and everybody was agreed that one of its first tasks would be to reform the Church. The air grew thick with apprehension; pamphlets fell like hail from the sky; everybody began forming plans for remaking the Church more nearly in accordance with his heart's desire. Schemes of well-meant redistribution of property and reorganization of worship and administration were put forward from all sides, except from that of the Church itself. Serious men anticipated that Parliament intended to enforce an ecclesiastical revolution. The immediate reactions to this crisis of the three great Oxford defenders of the faith were characteristic. Keble proposed to do nothing whatever until something should be actually pressed upon the Church which was contrary to its legal or customary rights. Pusey entered the lists of the pamphleteers with a remarkably able and far-seeing defence of cathedral endowments. Newman armed himself for battle by meditating on the apocalyptic visions of the book of Revelation. They were, however, exceedingly fruitful meditations.

Newman was wondering whether Constantine's

establishment of Christianity in the fourth century might not have been a disaster. Keble bluntly stated that anything was preferable to the Church of England continuing in association with such a State as that represented by the British Parliament. In February 1833 a Bill was introduced to amalgamate the Irish Bishoprics, and passed the Lords at the end of July. The turn of the English Church would follow. But by then resistance had come to a head. Keble, whose *Christian Year* was always reckoned both by Pusey and Newman to have been the original deposit of defensive piety from which the Oxford Movement was hatched, had to preach the University sermon before the Judge of Assize on 14th July. He delivered what seems to the modern reader a rather dull discourse on National Apostasy. But, if its effect appeared dull to contemporaries on its first publication, the dullness was only comparable to that produced on the ears by gunfire. The troops of Churchmanship had gone into action.

Events at last moved quickly. Pusey's old opponent, Rose, had already summoned certain stalwarts to a conference at Hadleigh. Keble and Newman were invited, but had no confidence in caucuses, and stayed away. But the idea of issuing some publications was broached, and the essential points singled out for defence were the Apostolical Succession and the integrity of the Prayer Book— precisely the two points which are threatened with attack to-day, not from Radical politicians, but from High Church Bishops. Hurrell Froude reported the proceedings to Oxford. Keble, Newman, and others then formed the 'Association of Friends of the Church,' of which the object was to 'maintain pure and inviolate the doctrines, the services, and the discipline of the Church.' Missionaries were dispatched and meetings held all over the country on similar lines, the most prominent organizer of the campaign being William Palmer, a liturgical scholar who had settled at Worcester College, Oxford. An address to the Archbishop of Canterbury, professing loyalty to Church principles, was signed by nearly seven thousand of the clergy in the next six months. A further address from the laity was presented shortly afterwards. The whole country was impressed by these events. For the time being the impending ecclesiastical revolution was brought to a stand.

Meanwhile the Newmanites, with Keble openly in support, had adopted the offensive. If Keble had converted Newman to sound Churchmanship, Newman had no less converted Keble to a policy of publicity. Together they formed a highly effective combination. Keble's union of principle, power, and delicacy rallied the educated Conservatives. Newman, with his faithful band of able young men, provided the means of startling the denizens of ecclesiastical backwoods and sedges into serious thought about the foundation truths of organized

Christianity. They both declined to believe that permanent salvation could be secured by the tired efforts of committees. Newman proposed the opening of a battery of short, sharp tracts, enforcing the essential points of Church polity. Keble agreed, and the first Tract for the Times appeared on 9th September.

Before the end of the year the Tracts numbered a score, half being written by Newman himself. Their tone is sufficiently described by Dean Church, who calls them 'clear, brief, stern appeals to conscience and reason, sparing of words, utterly without rhetoric, intense in purpose.' They recalled men to the teaching of the Caroline divines who had determined the character of the threatened Prayer Book at the Restoration, and of the primitive Fathers who were the theological masters of the Carolines. Moderates and committeemen were shocked at their outspokenness. Dignitaries were disconcerted to find themselves uncertain whether or not they believed the doctrines of the Church which they adorned. But the Tracts continued to pour from the press, and the country clergy read them with appreciation. A new force had been released among the varying currents of English religious life.

While all this activity was in progress Pusey held aloof. He was in sympathy with the demonstrators, but his time was still occupied with the Arabic catalogue, and perhaps also, as a dignitary himself, he may have felt at first that his place was in the judges' box rather than on the sand of the arena. He had not been invited either to Hadleigh or to the meetings at Oriel out of which the Association of Friends of the Church arose, nor did he join the Association. But he circulated Tracts, and signed the address to the Archbishop. Finally, on 21st December, the eighteenth Tract was issued with his initials, dealing at some length with the subject of fasting, which he recommended not only on grounds of obedience but still more by reference to practical wisdom and experience. This Tract committed him for good and all to the Tractarian cause.

Pusey's accession established the movement on a footing of respectability. As Newman said: "He at once gave to us a position and a name." He commanded great influence, not only in Oxford, but on many men outside, among whom were numbered people prominent in politics and society as well as in the Church. He was accordingly hailed as leader both by friends and opponents, and began to take some part, with Newman and Keble, in the direction of affairs, though he actually wrote few Tracts, and was not for some time anything like so deeply engaged in the campaign as his companions. It was not until the growth of opposition awoke his ever sensitive feelings of chivalry, that Pusey really assumed a joint leadership with Newman of the common cause.

For the time, the Tractarians, though disquieting to placid Oxford conservatism, were not unpopular. They proposed no innovations in religious practice, and their doctrinal arguments only sought, after all, to re-establish the truth of what the Prayer Book taught. Some Low Church fanatics might smell the sulphur of Popery in the Tracts, but the rulers of academic Oxford were not Low Church, and the expressed objective of the Tracts was against Popery and Dissent, with the suppression of both of which the University had every sympathy. In 1834 and 1835 Pusey played a leading part with non-Tractarian co-operators in resisting changes in the religious character of Oxford education. Dr. Hampden, who was opposed to all religious tests, was infuriated, but heavily defeated. But Newman was growing tired and discouraged. He began to despair of converting fellow-Churchmen who were capable of such crass ignorance and unfairness as to charge with Popery the defenders of Christian antiquity. The day was still to come when he would be convinced that the two things were identical, and join the Roman Church himself. In 1835 he proposed to discontinue the Tracts altogether. Then it was that Pusey contributed a weighty theological treatise on Baptism, in three Tracts, which changed the character of the movement. Hitherto the main object had been to arouse Churchmen to the fullness of their privileges and the glory of their heritage. They had been aroused. But the attitude of resentment in which certain of them had risen from their slumber disconcerted their principal awakener. Henceforward the movement was to aim at exposition of the foundations of Anglican principles; and Pusey moved up towards the van.

The Anglican Communion, as a reformed Church distinct from the Free Churches, has no other *raison d'être* in Christendom than to bear witness to the reality of sacramental grace; and Pusey realized that then, as now, the fight for sacramental grace was really a battle for continued belief in revelation and the Person of Christ. But great questions such as this can only be treated adequately on a grand scale, with full reference to Biblical theology and the ancient Church, and a thorough examination of the problem from all sides. From the publication of the work on Baptism, Pusey emerged as an unquestioned leader, and the movement took on the colour of a serious theological school, instead of a domestic controversy over the right interpretation of the Prayer Book. The earlier Tracts had roused attention. The later ones—for all idea of ceasing publication was promptly abandoned—attempted to give a carefully reasoned explanation and defence of the position adopted by the Tractarians. Such a change of attitude was indeed due to all honest enquirers. The true answer to accusations of Popery was by 'setting Catholic views against

Roman Catholicism and so disposing of Ultra-Protestantism by a side-wind.'

At this point the Regius Professorship of Divinity fell vacant, and the Prime Minister received from the Archbishop of Canterbury a long list of names of those who would be suitable to succeed to it. Pusey's name headed the roll; Newman appeared fourth in order, and Keble fifth. Acting on other advice, the Government ignored them all and appointed, early in 1836, the obnoxious Dr. Hampden. Oxford rang with indignation, in which the Tractarians joined, but were far from being the sole protesters. Hampden's theology amounted to a total disbelief in all theology, and reliance on the New Testament without creeds, sacraments, or authority. Such a position is less unfamiliar to-day than it was in 1836, but its advocates have even yet failed to square it with Anglicanism, to which the University was then committed. All Oxford ortho-doxy was involved in the conflict, but the leading part fell to Newman and Pusey, not because they were Tractarians, so much as because they were the men they were. Hampden and Hampdenism were condemned as emphatically as the University had power to condemn what had been thrust upon it by Government patronage. The controversy was un-dignified and regrettable, and had consequences most unfortunate for the Tractarians; the extreme Liberals never forgave them for their part in the affair, and nursed the opportunity for taking their revenge.

Foremost among the furious raged the famous Dr. Arnold, of Rugby, another former fellow of Oriel, and an old friend of Keble, who was godfather to his son Matthew. Sharing Hampden's opinions with equal ardour and greater intellectual ability, he based upon them a complete scheme for abolishing the practical distinction between Churchmanship and citizenship. As early as February 1834 Arnold had politely remonstrated with Pusey for lending his co-operation 'to a party second to none in the tendency of their principles to overthrow the truth of the Gospel.' But now he fairly gave his feelings their head. He stated that 'Newman and his party are idolaters,' 'conspirators,' propagating the 'fanaticism of mere foolery.' He divided them into two classes—the 'Hophni and Phinehas School,' consisting of the low, worldly, careless, and grossly ignorant; and the 'formalist Judaizing fanatics.' All this, and more, appeared in the *Edinburgh Review*. It would appear that the natural ferocity of a scholastic autocrat is insufficient to account for so venomous an outburst; such personalities are only open to the mind of a disappointed and defeated Radical politician.

Pusey's attention was merely turned to the need for publishing in an English translation certain of the actual works of the ancient Church Fathers,

with whom Arnold and Hampden so strongly disagreed, and whom the public to a large extent
imagined to have been Roman Catholics, simply
because they lived before the Reformation. The
Fathers were to Pusey's mind the true interpreters
alike of Holy Scripture, and of the formularies of the
Church of England. So Pusey and Newman made
the first arrangements for a series of translations, to
be called the *Library of the Fathers*, which finally
extended to nearly fifty volumes. Keble was brought
in to assist them in the work of editing; collaborators
were selected. The Bishop of London welcomed the
scheme. The Archbishop of Canterbury cordially
accepted the dedication of the series to himself. The
triumvirate appeared to be secure, if not yet
supreme. They had already an immense achievement on which to congratulate themselves. The
Church was certainly aroused. The Latitudinarians
were certainly defeated. The national religion was
saved from any serious danger of frontal assault.
The cause of theology and history was in the
ascendant.

At the same time the skies were not wholly fair,
even in quarters other than those from which Dr.
Arnold fulminated. The extreme Evangelicals perceived from the first that Tractarianism did not
chime with their subjective views of religion. As
early as in 1833 a Dr. Sikes, an old-fashioned High
Churchman, had pointed out in conversation that

the neglect then current of that article of the creed which refers to the Holy Catholic Church would some day be repaired, and prophesied that when that happened the Church would be unprepared. Those who should then teach it would be endlessly misunderstood; 'there will be one great outcry of Popery from one end of the country to the other.' At the very start of the Tracts, Pusey himself expected opposition and abuse. Before the Hampden controversy began the London *Standard* was denouncing High Churchmen as half-Papists, who, from the days of their parent, Laud, had rejected every principle consecrated by the blood of the Protestant Reformers; adding some graphic but grotesquely inaccurate personalities worthy of Dr. Arnold. In April 1836 a squib appeared which professed to be a pastoral from the Pope, addressed with approval to the authors of the Tracts. The forecasts of misinterpretation were being fulfilled. And from this time onward the attacks increased in virulence.

It was clear that serious trouble would have to be met, but so far there was no reason to apprehend its coming from others than the extreme Evangelicals and the extreme Liberals and Latitudinarians. Oxford was still more impressed than impatient at the deep moral earnestness of the movement. Outside, the Church authorities, though not converted, were not unsympathetic. Pusey had justification for the feelings of optimism which he entertained about the situation in the Church at large. A pilgrim from Cambridge to the Tractarian shrine wrote with enthusiasm of the things he saw and heard. The Doctor—Pusey took his D.D. in 1836—and Newman were said to govern the University. All the intellectuals sat at Newman's feet. Pusey, as well as Newman, drew vast congregations, and exercised an immense influence; those of the Oxford clergy who did not openly profess allegiance were imperceptibly adopting his sentiments. Such conclusions were in part exaggerated by the generous warmth of youthful partisanship ; but the impression remains that the cause was prosperous.

Chapter IV

PATERFAMILIAS

THE PUSEYS' ELDEST CHILD, Lucy, was born in 1829. Her father's deep sense of the happiness and responsibility of parenthood is illustrated by the fact that he continued to observe her birthday with special thanksgiving to the end of his life. Their only son, Philip, was born in the next year. Katherine saw the light of earth in January 1832 and left it in November. The stricken parents were upheld by a religious faith which impelled Pusey to write to his brother that only a true Christian can be a real optimist; what comes from a Father's love must be the best, even when it is most grave. They found human consolation in Keble's verses from *The Christian Year*, and in the friendship of Newman. Their youngest child, Mary, was born six months later.

As they were devoted lovers, so they were devoted parents. They both took immense pains with the education, especially the religious education, of their children. When one or other of the parents was away from home, their letters would devote a considerable space to the children's doings and progress. It was an age of stern discipline, when serious parents expected an unnatural seriousness of their tenderest offspring; and the Puseys both were very serious

44

people. The childish waywardnesses of the babies were a great grief to them. The punishments that they inflicted were probably most unwise, for the children were high-spirited and not robust. Still, to judge by results, excess of discipline is less harmful to character than it is to health, and it has taken another century for the discovery to be made that character does not matter by comparison. Curiously enough, it was the gay and laughing Maria who took the children's naughtiness most to heart, and the solemn and sober Edward who showed most appreciation of the fact that they were only babies after all. In spite of it all, the Puseys were a happy and devoted family.

A delightful picture survives from 1837 of the inmates of the Pusey household, in a letter, to which reference has already been made, from the Cambridge pilgrim to the professorial shrine at Christ Church. 'Presently, after dinner, Dr. Pusey's children ran into the room. One climbed Newman's knee and hugged him. Newman put his spectacles on him, and next on his sister, and great was the merriment of the Puseyan progeny.' Within the family dear J.H.N. had been meantime promoted to plain 'John.' How could it have been otherwise, when he was so devoted to the children? 'He told them a story of an old woman who had a broomstick which would go to the well, draw water, and do many things for her.' She grew tired of it, and

45

broke it in half. Imagine her dismay when, from the broken parts, *two* live broomsticks grew. Dear John. Dear children. What tragedies for all concerned lay just ahead.

Pusey's own health was none too good. He was seriously ill for four months in the winter of 1830, which he had to spend at Hastings; again in the autumn of 1833, and intermittently through the next year, being twice ordered off to the sea. The effect of ill-health on his introspective nature was to strengthen his sense of dependence on divine power, and to make him realize the necessity of setting some limit to his innumerable activities. He worked just as hard, but gave up several ambitious academic plans, in order to concentrate on the religious work which was of supreme importance. Spiritual interests came to supersede all that was of merely intellectual concern. It was apparently at this period, too, that his previous theological Liberalism imperceptibly merged into an affectionate reliance on the Fathers. Scripture remained paramount as ever in his mind. The question of authority related simply to its interpretation. The more he studied the Fathers, the more strongly he became convinced that they were truer interpreters of Scripture than modern writers; ancient Catholic truth better represented the meaning of the Bible than did modern private opinions. Recent tendencies in Biblical scholarship bear him out at least so far as this, that the New Testament is very widely regarded by critics of all schools as being essentially a Catholic compilation.

A week after their wedding, Jelf had written to Mrs. Pusey about her husband with the intimacy of an old friend. 'I rejoice to hear of the commencement of your despotism; the truth is, he is a child, quite unfit to be trusted with the management of his own health.' Maria was a true help-meet. Her devotion extended to the point of spending hours in the Bodleian library to assist him in the labours of patristic research. Pusey was as busy as he could be, producing sermons, pamphlets, tracts—not 'for the Times,' and, incidentally, rather bad ones—and writing vast numbers of letters to his many correspondents; in addition to his professorial teaching and the business of the cathedral chapter. Maria's task was not a light one. But she entered into all his occupations with a singular devotion, and, as she had once imparted to him her gift of cheerfulness at a time when he sorely needed it, so now she drew in turn from him a double portion of his own seriousness.

Her portrait shows her to have been a handsome woman, dressed to suit, with her hair worn in the fantastic waves and ringlets of the period. Her household maintained the dignity proper to her husband's position. But Edward had always hated luxury. The waste of idle fashion and self-indulgence appalled him. He was childlike in other matters than the care of his own health. Much as he was involved in controversy, he loathed the necessity; it was all so negative and destructive. Even Arnold, so late as 1838, wrote that: 'From Pusey you will learn, I am sure, nothing virulent, or proud, or false, but self-denial in its true form, combined with humility and honesty.' Consequently his charities were on a munificent scale. He helped to found a Hebrew scholarship at Oxford in 1832. In 1836 he was deeply concerned in the Bishop of London's plans for building churches for the growing population of his diocese. Pusey's own contribution, given anonymously, amounted to £5,000, though he was not a rich man. Although the Tractarians had defended the doctrine of the Church, declining to wage their warfare merely for its temporalities, they had opposed plans for diverting its ancient endowments. But they were keenly alive to the needs of the vast new urban populations brought into existence by the industrial revolution. In effect, Pusey's gift of £5,000 was an answer to the challenge that they were indifferent to the claims of the people to spiritual aid.

Here, too, Maria helped him. To meet the strain on their resources in 1837 they sold their horses and carriage. Maria sold all her jewellery. The proceeds went towards the London churches. Another scheme had been put into operation in the previous year.

They took four young graduates into their house as their guests, to study theology. The arrangement was thought to be queer, but it worked well. What their total benefactions came to cannot be conjectured, for most of them were done privately; but they were known to be very great. In his Tract on Fasting, Pusey had bidden men reflect on the glaring contrasts between luxury and misery. 'Let them only trace out one single item in the mass of human wretchedness, disease, insanity, religious ignorance, and picture to themselves what a Christian people might do, what the primitive Christians would have done, to relieve it'; then let them say whether any means of promoting self-denying charity can well be spared. It is fascinating to observe that such an interest in social problems marked the beginnings of the Oxford movement; these noble words proceed not from the Christian social movement, but from the pen of Edward Pusey in 1833. And what he preached, that he and Maria practised, with unobtrusive devotion.

But their wonderful partnership was drawing to an end. From 1835 as he grew stronger she became more delicate. Now it was she who had to be despatched to the sea, suffering from a persistent cough and fevers, which seem to indicate that she was consumptive. She rallied her strength somewhat after a long visit to the Channel Islands in 1837, but the improvement was short-lived, and at the end of the year her condition was grave. Then little Philip's health gave rise to serious anxiety; he recovered indeed, and lived for many years, but all his life he suffered physical disabilities that would have turned many into confirmed invalids, being very lame and very deaf. Mrs. Pusey grew steadily worse. The graduate students had to be lodged in another house. Still Pusey worked and planned and sacrificed, but in September 1838 it was recognized that his wife was beyond the aid of human skill. Again *The Christian Year* and his dear friends comforted him—and God. "I shall be so blessed," said Maria when he told her the doctors' verdict, "and God can make you happy." She lingered for another eight months. On 26th May 1839 he gave her Holy Communion for the last time. In the evening he made on her forehead the sign of the Cross, 'which she loved,' and blessed her; and she died. Another epoch in his life had ended.

Though the possibility had been before him for years and the practical certainty for months, yet, owing to his extreme sensibility and his introspective habit of reading a direct personal significance in all events that concerned him, Pusey was overwhelmed at his wife's death. He declined to see anybody. His mother, acting with the decision and the judgment of a Roman matron, sent straightway for Newman, who arrived within the hour. In thanking him for this visit, Pusey afterwards described it as having been to him "like that of an angel sent from God." There was grave need of such a visitant. Four years earlier, on the anniversary of the death of his infant daughter, Katherine, he had compared his loss to that of David when the child of Bathsheba died, regarding it as a chastisement for his own failure to achieve perfection. During Maria's last illness both Newman and Keble had felt obliged to write and warn him against treating it too much as a personal punishment for his own sins. Keble in particular forbade him to cherish feelings of excessive remorse. Newman now had to discharge the difficult and delicate task of directing his grief into wise and calm channels. It was the future, not the past, which most needed to be considered; he had to combat Pusey's self-depreciation and self-distrust with a reminder of the sufficiency of the grace of God. When it was all over, Pusey wrote to Keble with a deep thankfulness for the support which he had received; God had sent Newman to him; and again he said, "it was like the visit of an angel." So Newman, to whom Maria had once laughingly referred as 'St.' John, had his share in the making of a saint of Pusey.

For when Maria died, Pusey died with her to the satisfactions of this world. His sole interests henceforth bore a spiritual reference. He roused himself at once to work, without delaying beyond the day of his wife's funeral. But he was a changed man.

51

He reproached himself bitterly for the unsettling effects which he was led to attribute to his former work on the theology of Germany; the rest of his long life was to be spent in defence of revelation as he had now come to understand it, and in spiritual ministrations. His previous ascetic tendency was now intensified. He retired completely from society, in which he had once taken great delight. He could not even be persuaded to attend the domestic dinners of the cathedral chapter. The hour of Maria's departure he kept in daily remembrance. In walking from his lodging to the cathedral he kept his eyes on the ground, simply because he was unable to traverse the quadrangle across which the funeral procession had made its way, without recalling a vision of the white pall which had covered her coffin fluttering in the wind. While his labours and his charities continued, his personal austerity increased. The following details are drawn from a rule of life which he imposed on himself in 1846. He wore haircloth; he ate by preference unpleasant food; spectacles of natural beauty, which had always both attracted him and afforded him matter for religious comparisons, now provoked him to confess his own unworthiness; and when walking alone he spent the time in repeating the penitential Psalms. He made secret acts of humiliation when undergraduates or college servants touched their hats. The sight of the poor or neglected or degraded moved him to internal acknowledgments of inferiority. He made it his habit 'always to lie down in bed, confessing that I am unworthy to lie down except in hell, but so praying to lie down in the Everlasting Arms.'

For any one to imitate this line of conduct who had not received a definite vocation to anticipate in the course of his present existence something of the detachment and independence of creatures which belongs to the hereafter, would indeed be evidence of a morbid mind. Contempt of the world is not a wholesome object to pursue for its own sake alone. But Pusey was not morbid. On the contrary, his mind displayed a broad sanity, and his character a depth of spiritual reality, which might well be envied. The truth is that he walked with God so closely that all other interests were dwarfed and all other desires extinguished. His days were spent in prayer and work; sometimes his nights also. Even when he was seventy he used to labour on till midnight. When sixty, he usually rose at four o'clock, and celebrated the Holy Communion in his study, a privilege for which he had received the special permission of Bishop Wilberforce; and at seven a.m. he would be ready to welcome visitors with whom he used to make appointments for that early hour, or to engage on the other labours of the new day.

There was in this much that was heroic, but nothing morbid. It is true that he was concerned about his own soul, but the concern sprang from a conviction that good work could only proceed from a good workman. His first duty was to direct his own life aright, only in order that he might become a more useful instrument for the work of God to which he was called. That was from the first his express motive. His asceticism bore no trace of spiritual self-indulgence. His character was strengthened and not weakened by its practice. All the lovable qualities which had endeared him to his friends were deepened and intensified by his chastening of self. He had not retired into himself but into God. His gentleness, his lowliness, his reverence, his affection, all remained. His children, his friends, his fellow-men, and particularly the poor and friendless among them, continued to be the constant object of his care and love. But from the day of Maria's death he loved them all, not for himself but for God Who had entrusted them to his protection. In one word, he was a saint.

Forty years later, in writing to his youngest daughter about his feelings at the time of his loss, he said that he was unable to look either backward to the happiness of the past eleven years or forward to the intolerably emptied future. He seemed as if he were in deep water up to the chin, and God's hand under his chin supported him from day to day. He thought he could never smile again. But he took a holiday—still working—with the children; and although on the journey, while he was holding Philip up to look at Arundel Castle, the coach turned the sharp corner unexpectedly, and they both fell off on their heads, and Philip was stunned, they all reached Budleigh Salterton safely in the end; and there, with the children round him, he surprised himself in the strange act of smiling. His three little ones completed in him the work that Newman had been sent to begin.

But nobody can be a saint without being a penitent. And as a penitent, bringing forth fruits of repentance, he offered to build a church in the slums of Leeds, at the sole charges of his own economies, on the single condition that it should bear the inscription: 'Ye who enter this holy place, pray for the sinner who built it.' Like most of his gifts, this too was anonymous. He concealed the identity of the donor under the title of 'a person whom he knew,' 'his poor friend,' or the initial 'Z.' A site was secured next year. In 1842 the foundation-stone was laid, 'in the name of *Penitent*.' Poor Pusey was to have preached the sermon, but by that time the Tractarians had become the object of popular suspicion and hatred, and it was judged wiser that he should stay away. He bore with saintly meekness the deprivation of this satisfaction, and as the work slowly progressed took an immense interest in the details of the fabric and its furnishing. He hoped that it might be consecrated on Holy Cross Day, 1844, under the title of Holy Cross.

But in the spring of that year another blow fell on him. His eldest daughter, Lucy, had always been a delicate and sensitive child. She had felt her mother's death profoundly; even at that time Pusey had written: 'It may be that God is ripening her early, to close her trials soon.' She was deeply religious, looking forward keenly to her Confirmation, and actually receiving it at what was then the unusually early age of twelve, in 1841. She sympathized intimately with all her widowed father's religious hopes and efforts, and after her Confirmation formed the intention of devoting herself in person to one purpose that lay very near his heart, the revival in the English Church of sisterhoods for the care of Christ's sick and poor. To Pusey she represented the embodiment of his wife's love and his own religious aspirations. Now she, too, was stricken with consumption, following an attack of whooping-cough. In less than three weeks she too had passed away.

Before she died she expressed a wish that a sum of forty pounds belonging to her should be spent on some gift for the service of the altar in the new church at Leeds. In accordance with her desire Pusey proposed a chalice, with an inscription incorporating a prayer for Lucy, and offered a second himself. The Leeds church, which was the outward symbol of the dedication of his sorrow, thus became intertwined with a new grief. But difficulty after difficulty arose. Legal objections were made to the intended form of the altar; it was a matter of principle with Pusey that God's board should not be a mere common table, but the ecclesiastical courts had just laid down the illegality of stone altars, and Pusey had to acquiesce in a wooden one. Then the Bishop suddenly discovered a dislike for the dedication to Holy Cross; to please him it was altered to St. Saviour, though Lucy, like her father, had a great devotion for the Cross of Christ. The suspicious prelate next objected to a window in which there was to be a representation of the Face of Our Lord; he had already been shown the drawings, and returned them without criticism; but when a prejudiced and partisan episcopate is really jealous for its faith there is no end to its capacity for detailed interference. Pusey replied that the Bishop could put in plain white glass instead if he were so minded, and commended the whole matter to Our Lord, for whose glory it was meant.

In August 1845 the Bishop flatly declined to consecrate the church at all if the chalice with Lucy's name on it were in the building, for fear that he should be thought to countenance the Christian habit of asking the blessing of God on the beloved dead. So the chalice was kept back, and not presented till the next year, with a compromise effected over the inscription. At last the day of consecration drew near, in October, 1845. Three weeks earlier dear J.H.N. had been received into the Roman Church; Pusey was bereft of his dearest companion and the closest counsellor of his earlier days, and England seethed with patriotic anti-Roman fervour. The Bishop was stirred to a fresh outburst of cautious zeal, condemning three sections of the west window, the Cross over the chancel screen, and even the comparatively innocuous altar linen, which had been specially worked for the church. Pusey left him to this pious reformation without remonstrance; but his mother was moved to observe that the Bishop would have saved both expense and vexation to the family if he had disclosed his scruples earlier. Finally, on the very day before the consecration, the Bishop ordered the inscription, on condition of which the gift of the church had been originally made and accepted by his lordship, to be obliterated forthwith, for fear that the founder therein to be prayed for might be already dead. However, on being assured that the founder was yet alive, and on receipt of an undertaking that he should be informed in case of the donor dying while he himself remained in occupation of the See, he permitted the ceremonies to proceed without breach of faith. Though vexatious, he was just, according to his lights.

So, after many disappointments, the meekness, generosity, and forbearance of Pusey triumphed; he was allowed to see his church completed, and to read on its fabric the words which he had chosen: 'Pray for the sinner who built it.' Maria was dead, and Lucy was dead, and Newman was worse than dead to his beloved Church of England. Little Philip, owing to increasing physical infirmities, was shortly to be compelled to renounce his desire to be a priest like his father. But he still had two dear children with him, and dear J.K. at Hursley behind him; and beneath him were the everlasting arms. He stood bereaved and vilified, but secure and calm and grateful in his faith. In the hope of making things easier for Dr. Hook, the Vicar of Leeds, who had once been a fellow-undergraduate with him at Christ Church, he had even offered to stay away from the consecration of St. Saviour's; but to Hook's everlasting credit, in spite of many evidences of nervousness and vacillation, he refused to hear of any such suggestion. The consecration was a most impressive function. Two hundred and sixty clergy attended, and the church was packed. The service lasted nearly five hours. Pusey preached a sermon in the evening, and for a whole week two or three sermons were delivered every day, half by Pusey of his own composition, most of the rest by him as deputy for other famous priests who, after writing them for the occasion, had been prevented by different reasons from being present. The mission aimed at enforcing the realities of the unseen world, and leading the hearers through repentance to hope. As always, the lessons which Pusey had learned through the intensity of his personal trials he could not selfishly reserve to his own soul, but had to pass on to his brother men.

Chapter V

OUTCAST

IT MUST ALWAYS BE REMEMBERED that the Tractarian movement was originally anti-Roman. The Tracts were directed in support of the doctrine of the Church of England against Popery and Dissent. Popular ignorance, saturated with the extreme individualism of the Evangelicals, and warped through the exaggerated insistence laid on subjective emotion by Methodists who had forgotten the sacramental teaching and practice of their founders, made the not unnatural mistake of confusing the doctrine of Churchmanship with Roman Catholicism. Newman had almost despaired; but Pusey came to the rescue with the heavy theology. Another consequence of the character of the opposition was that Newman was induced to write some Tracts expressly 'against Romanism,' and devoted much of 1836 to his important *Lectures on the Prophetical Office of the Church*, published the next year, in which the Roman position was severely criticized. The Hampden controversy, which occurred just at this time, brought on the Tractarians the rancour of the Liberals, but since Oxford as a whole rejoiced to see the Liberals defeated, the position of the movement in its academic headquarters remained unaffected by any emission of Latitudinarian chlorine.

At the same time, suspicions began to grow at Oxford. The dominant party in the university was made up for the most part of 'complacent, unlearned and pompous folk, given chiefly to politics and the pleasures of the table.' They were prepared to accept as allies, when it suited them, the keen, ascetic, serious-minded Tractarians, but they had no fellow-feeling for them. Pusey had graduated into public life as something of a radical; now he was given over to a form of religious 'enthusiasm,' which might be all the more dangerous because it was new. He was respected, but feared. He was also a young man, and Tories dread youth, because the young are apt to demand novelty both in men and in measures, and sometimes agitate for the replacement of accepted conventions, and even of existing leaders. The Oxford standpoint may be illustrated by an incident which occurred a little later. Pusey was required to give evidence in a case of alleged lunacy, and counsel asked him whether a person who gave away very large sums of money to religious objects could be reckoned fit to manage property. As this indiscretion was exactly what Pusey had committed, he gravely replied that such a person might be considered capable. But the Oxford Conservatives would have given a different answer.

Their attitude to Newman was quite distinct, and much more hostile. Even the Keble School was shocked at his 'habit of looking for effect.' Pressure was put on the reticent J.K. to publish, 'in order to keep pace with Newman and so maintain a more practical turn in the movement.' People were scared of his brilliance; they did not want cleverness, but the steady sobriety of the Keble standpoint. When friends thus doubted, it is easy to infer the feelings of opponents. And Newman was not merely an ex-Liberal, like Pusey, but an ex-Evangelical. His old friends hated him for deserting them, while his new academic allies despised him for the traces which he still bore strongly marked on his mind of his old loyalties. The ardour of his young disciples was an added offence. Newman had become the leader of a band of partisans, in fact, an agitator. Moreover, his disciples had less discretion than their chief. Changes which they were anxious to introduce in the outward observances of religion, minute in themselves, and universally accepted to-day, were the occasion of horrified outcry. In 1837 Pusey had his work cut out to defend them to the Bishop of Oxford. The young Newmanite clergy were accused of indulgence in 'needless bowings.' Pusey said he knew of none such performed, except those (ordered by the Canons) to be made at the Name of Our Lord. One daring individual positively wore an unpretending Cross embroidered at the two ends of his black scarf, as is common on the modern stoles normally worn by clergy engaged on various public ministrations. Pusey defended this as an attempt to

63

obey the Ornaments Rubric of the Prayer Book; adding that 'a rigid adherence to the Rubric cannot in its own nature, lead to extravagance, and it seemed a very safe way for the exuberance of youth to vent itself in.' But he felt obliged to state his own willingness to acquiesce in a more lax interpretation of the rule. His own standard of the relative importance of such things is clear. "We have too much to do to keep sound doctrine and the privileges of the Church to be able to afford to go into the question about dresses." The innovations for which this apology had to be made were modest indeed. But they were innovations. And there was no knowing where the most unpretending change might end, especially when it embodied the Cross of Christ, then accepted as the domestic badge of the Scarlet Whore of Rome. So Holy Week of 1837 was signalized at Oxford by the decoration of the walls with placards, denouncing Popery and condemning Newman and Pusey by name as Papists.

The premature death of Hurrell Froude, in February 1836, conveyed an unrecognized foretoken of disaster to the movement. It left a void in Newman's heart which Pusey could not fill. Profound as was the love between them, coming events showed that Newman entirely failed to penetrate to the deeper levels of his friend's mind; on the other side, Pusey did not joke and scoff, and the paradoxical truth appears to present itself, that Newman

the intellectualist was better able to be guided by
the whip of scorn than by the sober reins of
practical reason. Little as anybody realized in 1836,
Froude's death severed the rope which held Newman to his anchorage, and left his susceptible mind
open to the influence of dangerous cross-currents.
It also gave occasion to the most serious trouble
which the Tractarians had as yet encountered.
Froude left behind him journals and other papers
which expressed his deep convictions with characteristic force and humour. These were collected and
published, together with reminiscences of his conversation, by Keble and Newman in 1838 and 1839.
The work was undertaken both as a pious memorial
to an exceptionally gifted friend, and as a bold
illustration of the 'awful reality of devotion,' and
the critical strength, which underlay the whole
Tractarian movement. But the result was to precipitate a first-class crisis. Froude had spoken with
levity and disrespect of the sacred Reformation, and
called the Elizabethan Bishop Jewel 'an irreverent
dissenter.' England howled with indignation
throughout its reactionary coils.

The editors had been too honest to be politic:
and Pusey was too loyal to stand aside from the
ensuing *mêlée*. He protested that the Tractarians
neither promoted nor desired any change in the
formularies of the Church; they only wished to act
up to the standards which the formularies contained.

At the same time, he thought the outcry might do good. The spread of the movement had been too rapid; a check might be salutary, forcing men back on principles, and disciplining the exuberance of some of the younger partisans. When the Bishop of Oxford included in his charge of 1838 some mild criticism of the Tract-writers, which suggested that they lacked appreciation of the need for caution in instructing others younger than themselves, Newman was again depressed and suggested withdrawing all the Tracts from circulation; but Pusey proceeded to tackle the Bishop and extracted from him a sympathetic denial that he intended to censure rather than to counsel. Pusey, as always, exercised a mediating and moderating influence on men of goodwill. Under his pilotage the storms of the year were weathered, and early in 1839 he produced, by arrangement with the Bishop, an 'open' letter to the Bishop of Oxford, running to over two hundred printed pages, in which he repudiated the charges of Popery brought against the movement, and showed that the Tractarians, together with the official Church of England, held a distinct line, 'removed from modern novelties, whether of Rome or of ultra-Protestantism.' If Papists rejoiced at the revival of Church principles in England, their satisfaction was premature; if ultra-Protestants attacked the Tracts as Popish, it showed their grave misunderstanding both of Popery and of the Tracts.

But for all that, Newman had received a nasty blow. He retained all the Evangelical's demand for personal assurance; reason and judgment dealt so much with probabilities, and he could not proceed in comfort on his course without some Living Voice to confirm him in the hope that he was right. Having discarded the Evangelical conception that the necessary Living Voice resided in his own emotions, and, being disappointed in the expectation of finding it in popular approval, he now looked to his ecclesiastical superiors to supply it. While Pusey relied on the principles and doctrine of the Church of England as sufficient warranty for his own teaching, Newman relied on his power to convince the Bishops. And at this first semblance of condemnation by the new Living Voice which he had chosen, he had been thrown into a flutter. It was an ominous forecast of the day when he should be compelled to change his Living Voice for the last time and seek assurance from the Pope.

1839 was the year of Pusey's private tragedy, and the central turning-point of his whole life. But it also marked the true crisis of the Church of England in relation to the Oxford movement. No one who knew him—except the sanguine Newman—ever dreamed that Pusey would or could become a Roman Catholic. If the movement had been in his hands alone, fears and suspicions might have been dissipated. But his co-director was very differently regarded. And it was in 1839 that two events occurred which led to the further undermining of Newman's faith in the Church of England. One was theological. An article by the Roman Bishop Wiseman, supervening on his own studies in ecclesiastical history, suddenly raised a dreadful spectre in his mind that Anglicanism might be only another heretical throw-out in the course of Western Catholic development, like Monophysitism (as he understood it) in the sixth century and Donatism in the fourth; was the Church of his fathers simply a monstrous birth on a by-path of the triumphant march of Catholic and Roman Christianity? The other was personal. A former disciple of Arnold, W. G. Ward, from reading the *Remains* of Hurrell Froude, was converted to Newmanism. Ward in many ways resembled Froude. He was as uncompromising, brilliant, and attractive; but far more reckless and irresponsible, less indeed of a daring critic than an impassioned controversialist. He was quite unconvinced of the possibility of regenerating the Church of England, and aimed at a complete disavowal, not merely of certain of the Protestant Reformers, but of the principles of the Reformation. And it was he who now began to fill the void in Newman's heart left by the death of Froude.

The process of Newman's unsettlement was

completed by the uproar which attended the publication of *Tract 90* in February 1841. In this able piece of historical criticism, of which Keble whole-heartedly approved both the substance and the publication, Newman maintained 'that the Thirty-nine Articles ought to be subscribed in the literal and grammatical sense; but I maintained also that they were so drawn up as to admit, in that grammatical sense, of subscription on the part of persons who differed very much from each other in the judgment which they formed of Catholic doctrine.' That was his considered statement of his aims, made in 1863. Later historical research has proved him right. But three facts combined to annihilate him in contemporary estimation. Popular opinion was rabidly intolerant of anything which appeared to be even remotely associated with any part of the religious system professed by the Roman Church, and was convinced that Newman's proof of a toleration of Catholic teaching in the Articles wider than that accepted in recent tradition was simply evidence of his Romanizing; he was, in fact, dishonest. The Bishops were dreadfully alarmed at the intensification of controversy; Newman was splitting the Church. A little later the reckless Ward proclaimed that for his own part he subscribed the Articles in a non-natural sense; and Oxford with savage gratification began to hear rumours of threatened defections. The fat was in the fire, and the fire was blazing.

The immediate consequence was that *Tract 90* was censured by the Heads of Houses at Oxford, and practically every Bishop in England started to issue charges condemning the Tractarians, certain of them in strongly vituperative language, which was unfortunate for a movement which had done so much to reassert episcopal authority. It was agreed to publish no more Tracts. Pusey interviewed the Archbishop of Canterbury (Howley), who was almost the only Bishop that kept his head or showed any understanding of the position; years afterwards Pusey acknowledged with gratitude that Howley "alone never censured us." But another blow was to descend on the shattered forces of Churchmanship. Later in the year Parliament sanctioned the establishment of an Anglo-Prussian bishopric in Jerusalem, which was to minister to British Anglicans and German Lutherans in the Levant. Pusey was at first sympathetic, seeing in the proposal a possible means of drawing Lutherans into episcopacy; later he perceived that the plan was mainly political, and that the ordination of Lutherans who did not believe in priesthood or episcopacy was a doctrinal sham. But to the Newmanite view the proposal simply drove another nail into the coffin of the reformed Catholic Church of England. Ultimately the scheme did nothing to promote reunion, and little for anyone except to help in making Newman a Papist. It came to an end in 1881.

Newman retired with his friends to Littlemore, two miles out of Oxford, and a few secessions took place—enough to confirm the worst suspicions of the enemy. Early in 1842 Pusey reviewed the whole situation in another 'open' letter, addressed to the Archbishop. He accounted for the Romeward tendency by the recent growth of the Roman Church in England, independently of the Tracts, and by the desire for visible unity with fellow-Catholics. He deplored the partiality and misunderstanding of the episcopal charges, which had loosed a flood of profanity and unsettlement on the whole Church of England. He asserted the truth, that the leaders had never sought to draw people towards themselves, but to the system of the Church. He pointed out that the probable effect of the attacks would be to drive the despondent and impatient into the arms of Rome. But the harm had been done. In January 1843 Newman wrote a retractation of all the hard things which he had ever said of the Roman Church. Pusey tried to persuade himself that this was merely due to charity. Others rightly saw in it a deeper significance.

Pusey would not believe that Newman intended to secede to Rome, and did his utmost to counteract the tendencies which urged him thither. He stressed the great revival of Church life, not only in England but throughout the Anglican communion, as an evident sign that God was with the English Church. He continued to consult Newman about practical details, particularly about the holding back of men who were on the brink of secession. He defended him against his detractors and wished that he himself might have been the one selected to bear the burden of the persecution. Newman, on his part, could not bear to undeceive Pusey so long as a glimmer of hope remained. But he knew in his own mind that he would go to Rome, and Keble, who had been for several years his closest confidant, knew it, too. What Newman was waiting for was simply, as before, personal assurance. The present source to which he was looking for a guiding sign was the providential direction of public events; and unfortunately each successive public event only accumulated further grounds for doubting that the Church of England was truly Catholic. All the signals that impressed him pointed Romewards.

In May 1843 Pusey preached a very ordinary sermon, based on the teaching of the ancient Fathers, on the Holy Eucharist. Two days later the university was astonished to hear that the preacher had been delated to the Vice-Chancellor for heresy. He was to have his wish fulfilled and join the ranks of the unjustly persecuted. The whole affair, which is very fully treated in Liddon's *Life of Dr. Pusey*, was conducted in a manner highly discreditable to his accusers. Pusey (like Newman, so far) was condemned unheard; and by prejudiced judges; and in general terms, not on specified counts. He was tricked, in the simplicity of his heart, into making a promise to refrain from any public defence, or even from publication of the secret documents that passed between him and his accusers. He was not even allowed to consult his friends. And as soon as he had passed his word, he was sentenced to be suspended from preaching in the university for two years. Every effort which he made to appeal either to secular or to ecclesiastical courts was frustrated. It was another signal defeat for the Tractarian cause. On Pusey himself the effect was negligible. At the expiration of the two years he stood up again in the University pulpit and quietly repeated the substance of the condemned sermon, and nobody dared take any action. The purpose of the condemnation had been served. But the unfairness of the proceedings shocked the younger school of Liberals, led by Tait, afterwards Archbishop of Canterbury, and by destroying all confidence in the administration of the university paved the way for university reform. And it afforded yet another sign to the depressed and expectant hermit of Littlemore. Before the next term opened he had resigned the vicarage of St. Mary's.

The Bishop of Winchester declined to license Keble's curate. The Bishop of Chester formally ascribed the movement to the energies of Satan. A Cheltenham cleric, afterwards rewarded with the deanery of Carlisle, publicly stated that he would not trust the author of *Tract 90* with his purse.

Ordination candidates were cross-examined on a variety of subjects, including their attitude to that famous Tract. Newman celebrated his last Anglican Eucharist at St. Mary's, and preached his last Anglican sermon at Littlemore. "O my mother," he cried in his distress to the Church of England, "whence is this unto thee, that thou hast good things poured upon thee and canst not keep them, and bearest children, yet darest not own them?" The audience sobbed openly, and Pusey, who was celebrating, scarcely refrained from mingling tears with the Sacrifice. But still he hoped. Even a year later, when Newman told him explicitly what the event would be, he tried to put the best construction on the melancholy facts. Newman was still in lay communion, still seeking a clinching sign; and he could not utterly despair.

Meantime other secessions took place. Ward was writing more defiantly and aggressively than ever. Finally, in June 1844 he published his *Ideal of a Christian Church*, underlining every shortcoming in the Anglican system, and claiming the right to hold the whole cycle of Roman doctrine. Still the loyal and generous Pusey tried to make the best of things, and defended the aggressor so far as he honestly could. But the enemy had determined to take the chance offered by Ward's recklessness and the general consternation which it occasioned in the Church, to strike a smashing blow. The Convocation of the University was summoned to meet in February 1845, in order to pass three propositions. The first condemned Ward's book and good faith in writing it. The second stripped him of his degrees. The third, introduced at the last moment, condemned *Tract 90*.

The third was vetoed by the proctors, of whom one was Church, afterwards Dean of St. Paul's; but the carriage of the other two provided sign enough for Ward's master. Ward himself was unabashed. His original but effective method of expressing contempt for the bites of academic mosquitoes was to announce his engagement to be married. Pusey protested against the inveterate onesidedness of the authorities in the Church, who persecuted extravagance in one direction while they ignored more serious excesses or negligences in the other. But nothing now could either save Newman or bring the Bishops to see reason. One by one the Newmanites seceded, their leader holding out until October. When he went, Pusey promptly poured out his heart in a letter to the press. He spoke of his overwhelming sorrow at the event, ascribing it to lack of prayer and faith among Anglicans. He suggested that God had some deep purpose for Newman in the Roman Church, as an instrument of spiritual revival—a suggestion not immediately fulfilled, but even yet not utterly impossible of indirect and ultimate fulfilment. And he pointed once again to the wonderful growth of life and vigour during the past ten years in the English Church; all this was not the work of the Tractarians, but of God. So Pusey, who was neither Pope nor prelate, but a true Peter, stablished his brethren.

Newman, dazzled by his new experience and deafened, perhaps, by the emphatic tones of his last-discovered Living Voice, hoped for nine months to induce Pusey to follow his example. He little knew his man, and his persistence caused a silent break in the communications of the old familiar friends. Pusey remained, with the support of Keble and lesser leaders, to bear the brunt of the explosion, binding up the limbs broken in the catastrophe, and healing the wounds episcopally inflicted. Tractarian principles gradually came to meet with widespread acceptance. It is largely to Pusey's wide and lasting influence that this result is due. Less satisfactory is the fact that the external symbols of Catholicity, under other influences, have become the common-place insignia of many who do not share the belief of Pusey and Keble. Sometimes a fair mitre covers the head of one who denies the Apostolical succession for which they contended and endured. If they were to rise from the dead, there would still be work in plenty to their hands.

Chapter VI

VIA CRUCIS

NEWMAN HAD CALLED THE COURSE which he attempted to steer, between Popery and Protestantism, the *Via Media*, or Middle Way. Pusey was now finding it a *Via Crucis*, or Way of the Cross. Again and again he insisted that the object of the Tractarian Movement had never been to draw people towards its leaders or to form a party, but to recall Churchmen to the teaching of their Church. The great fault of the Tractarians, especially of Newman, because he was the most active centre of personal discipleship, was that they did not lead. Instead, in their horror of putting themselves forward, they allowed Ward, 'like Phæton with the chariot of the sun,' to take the reins out of Newman's hands, with similarly disastrous consequences. Always they looked to the bishops for leadership. From the first they had appealed to the Church to rally to the bishops. But the bishops wholly misunderstood and misjudged the movement, as politically appointed bishops have done in similar circumstances at other times with singular fidelity to type. 'I speak from personal knowledge,' wrote Pusey in 1874, 'when I say that the Bishops might have guided the Movement of 1833, etc., if they would. There was nothing that we who were young then, so much wished.'

Instead of leading the movement, the bishops hounded Newman and his associates into the arms of Rome. And like Herod Agrippa, having slain James with the sword and observed how their action delighted the mob, they now attempted to take Peter also.

Pusey hated controversy. He knew how it tended to lower the spiritual tone of the disputants. He was forced into it against his will; striving always to avoid asperities, yet still hating his position. Five days after Newman's secession, Samuel Wilberforce was appointed Bishop of Oxford. The new bishop, though he had known Pusey for years, was convinced that Pusey was leading people to Rome, and promptly wrote, before he was even enthroned, accusing Pusey of dangerous self-will and disloyalty to the Church of England. After that, it was a mere nothing that the Vice-Chancellor of Oxford told Pusey that he was lacking in spiritual discernment. The general attitude may be judged from a few facts. Some of the Heads of Houses refused to speak to him when they met him in the street. His Oxford friends visited him by stealth; his mere acquaintance was regarded as damning. Every post brought letters, some signed, others anonymous, reflecting on his honesty or his intelligence. Old allies of the High Church order became distant if they did not positively denounce him. He was 'a ravening wolf from the banks of the Isis,' and 'wandered about as an ecclesiastical Cain, with the Vice-Chancellor's mark on his forehead, and an Exeter Hall anathema on his head.' The very school at Clifton which his daughters attended suffered loss of pupils from its innocent connexion with their father.

Some proportion of the public suspicion and hatred might have been averted if Pusey had done as certain of his advisers wished, and published a vigorous attack on Popery and on Newman for becoming a Papist. But this he consistently refused to consider. How could he? He loved Newman, and every impulse of his chivalrous soul impelled him rather to defend and explain than to vituperate. And greatly as he misliked various comparatively modern features in the Roman system, what was good and true in the teaching of the Church of Rome far outweighed her mediæval and modern corruptions: it will be remembered that Romanism in England still bore the brand of Bishop Challoner, not that of Pius IX and Archbishop Manning. If it came to a comparative estimate of corruption and falsity to principle, how could any Anglican throw the first stone? The proper attitude for the Church of England was one of penitence, not of arrogance; the twelve years that had passed since the movement opened had brought that fact into emphatic prominence. So he declined to bay with the pack. In print and pulpit he maintained a 'public neutrality.' In private, not a day passed but he gave his counsel to those who asked him, either by word or correspondence, against the exclusive claims of Rome, which, if allowed, would have made of his mother, the Church of England, a harlot.

His great desire was to be left alone, with his professorial teaching, with his folios of Fathers of the Church, with his nation-wide 'parish' of spiritual ministration to hundreds who relied on him for guidance and means of grace. But any such desire was quite impossible of fulfilment. He was the target of well-nigh universal censure and abuse; the lone column, as a uniquely rational Protestant writer described him, remaining from the ruin of a once stately portico. Most of England waited day by day to hear that he, too, had fallen. The pitiful remainder leaned on him, and he had to lend them active support. A year after the catastrophe he wrote about his over-work and the illness which it had brought on in the autumn of 1846. "I was worn out; I laboured often night as well as day; I had not a feeling of health for more than a year of toil and sorrow. I felt that I could not stand it. But what could I do? God brought me at that crisis work to do, often thankless; I cast away everything, so that I might, by God's mercy, retain children of our Church within her. What the extent of misgivings was then, you probably can never know"—he was writing to Hook, who, with the rest, had turned against him. "I speak strictly when I say that people (clergy also) seemed (in the language of Holy Scripture) 'like the ripe fig, ready to drop into the mouth of the eater'; they were panic-stricken; and as men in a panic, needed to be reassured."

The spirit in which he conducted the overwhelming work of reassurance may be illustrated by the words of the uniquely rational Protestant just referred to, in describing a sermon which Pusey preached in a village church. "Never before did I hear so beautifully evangelical a sermon as this. . . . It was listened to throughout by that little crowded church-full with fixed and rapt attention, though it was neither declamatory, noisy, nor eccentric; but plaintive, solemn, and subdued, breathing throughout, I may say, a beauty of holiness and a Christian spirit so broad and catholic, so deep and devotional, that while the most zealous Protestant could find nothing in it he might not approve, the most bigoted Roman Catholic could not enter an exception to a single expression that it contained." "There he stood, a plain, and, to all appearance, an humble and lowly man, preaching to a simple people, and speaking with the melancholy meekness as of one stricken and tried, yet uncomplaining"; and delivered a sermon "more perfectly free from controversy than ever I before heard." " 'Who be that that preached?' said one young rustic maiden to another as we left the church; 'a monstrous nice man, but dreadful long.'—'Don't you know?' replied the other; 'it is that Mr. Pewdsey, who is such a friend to the Pope; but come along, or we'll be late for tea'; and away they trotted."

Pusey had been hearing confessions since about 1838 and well knew the benefits of that means of grace, particularly to young men. He owned that he believed the prejudice being diligently sown against it to be "purely the work of the devil." He had not sought his penitents; they simply came to him and demanded the rights which the Prayer Book offered them. In February 1846 he had preached on the subject to the University, and for some time past had desired to make his own confession, but had till now been hindered by considerations which he thought valid. However, in December 1846 he went to Hursley and made his first confession to Keble; and after that until Keble's death he made the journey at least three times every year for the same purpose. "Penitent thyself thou shalt learn to speak to the hearts of penitents. Thou knowest too well the wounds which enter the soul; thou wilt know the healing wherewith the Great Physician shall have healed thee." Thus he preached that which he now began to practise. How deep the healing power went in his own soul may be judged from the fact that he ever after addressed J.K. in his letters as 'My dearest Father.'

To this form of address Keble's first reply began: 'My dearest Friend, and Son that ought to be

Father, and something more than I can say——'
and at that he broke off. The love between them
was a thing beyond verbal expression. Whatever
storms might break over his head, Pusey always had
one sure refuge on earth in dear J.K. There were
other loyal friends, even at this stony period of his
pilgrimage, such as Charles Marriott, his devoted
ally in Oxford, who took off his shoulders after
1843 much of the burden of editing the *Library of the
Fathers*, and assisted him in countless services of
friendship and learning; practically succeeding to
the place in the Tractarian movement which Newman had vacated. But to none could he so turn, and
to none was he so bound, as to dear J.K. They consulted over every matter of importance. When
Pusey was the victim of some specially virulent or
dangerous attack, it was J.K. who rushed to the
defence, against all his natural inclination towards
retirement. "Remember," he would say with emphatic vigour to detractors, "I am a 'Puseyite' of the
very deepest dye." When the slightest difference of
opinion arose between them on a question of policy,
they were both thrown into fits of distress—though they
never differed seriously or for long about anything.
When Pusey was diffident, it was J.K.'s advice which
spurred him on and strengthened his resolution. In all
the long tradition of human history there are few
instances of a pair of saints so finely matched, so
closely knit, or possessing such a spiritual beauty.

Dignitaries and ecclesiastical proletariate alike were waiting vengefully for Pusey to succumb and follow Newman. The first deadly blow was struck at him through the monument of his sorrows, St. Saviour's, Leeds. Hook, a man of excitable and impetuous judgment, though a devout and earnest priest, entirely lost his head and accused Pusey of having planted 'a colony of Papists' in the heart of Leeds. He refused any longer to sign himself 'yours affectionately.' Then he refused to correspond at all: Pusey was, he alleged, stabbing him under the fifth rib with a smile on his face. From the end of 1846 until April 1851 the unfortunate parish and its clergy were harried by Hook and the no less devastating Bishop of Ripon, who had already proved his destructive qualities before the consecration. The vicar was forced to resign, and great difficulties were placed in the way of the apppointment of a successor. Finally Hook and the bishop fairly drove most of the clergy, past and present, of the parish into the Roman obedience, and the work was reduced twice over to a spiritual wreck. Even then most of the laity stood firm in their Anglicanism. Pusey went down to preach in 1851 and fainted in the church. But he was able to write home to Philip, 'I am well again, and amid much sorrow have had much comfort. It has been a new scene to me. Boys, mechanics, and mill-girls, using confession; kneeling thankfully for the blessing, and bound to the Church by a stronger bond than that which bound them to their late pastors.' People would not see it, but clinching evidence was there that Pusey not only loved the Church of England with a loyal devotion, but was leading others to a like constancy.

In 1848 Archbishop Howley died. The choice of his three successors, who between them covered exactly the remaining period of Pusey's life, indicates the amount of sympathy felt in Governmental and official circles for the views with which Pusey was identified. The first of the trio was Dr. Sumner, that Bishop of Chester who had called the Tractarians 'instruments of Satan to hinder the true principles of the Gospel.' The second was Dr. Longley, whom we have twice met as Bishop of Ripon in connexion with St. Saviour's, Leeds. The third was Dr. Tait, of the younger Evangelical school, a disciple of Dr. Arnold, an unflinching opponent of Tractarianism, and one of the four Oxford tutors who in 1841 had started the attack on *Tract 90*. It may be said with truth that in all those years the See of Canterbury did little to promote the cause of Churchmanship, for which Pusey offered his life in penitential sacrifice. Yet he, and not they, prevailed—the 'plain and apparently unpretending man, of mild manners and of middle years and stature,' against the captains and the big battalions. The fact is worthy of consideration both by those who follow and by those who still oppose him.

The opposition of the Bishops was in part accompanied, and in part was caused, by the offence and odium first incurred by Newman, then perversely generated in bulk by Ward, and finally transferred to Pusey as a scapegoat. The atmosphere thus created made impartial judgment an impossibility. The one fact which throws a brighter light on the situation during the ten years after Newman's secession is that the translations from ancient Church writers, published in the *Library of the Fathers*, continued to gain subscribers. The appeal to history thus claimed attention, though its fruits were not as yet apparent. The series began in 1838 with less than a thousand subscribers. In 1843 this number had risen to nearly eighteen hundred, including twenty-five bishops, though it is not stated how many of their twenty-five copies of each issue remained uncut. By 1851 the figures were nearly two thousand five hundred, with twenty-nine bishops; and two years later, after a public appeal by Pusey, the subscribers exceeded three thousand seven hundred. The figures show that solid foundations were now, as ever, being laid by the Tractarian leaders, and that the loyal remnant of the movement was rallying from the shock of '45. Two prominent archdeacons supported the cause: Robert Wilberforce, elder brother of the great Samuel, the new Bishop of Oxford; and Henry Edward Manning, a thrusting ex-Evangelical, who already in

1847 was expressing to Pusey his misgivings that the direct and certain tendency of what remained from the original movement was towards the Church of Rome. The Church of England was inclosed in bounds too strait for the survivors— Manning does not as yet say that they were too strait for himself.

The next controversy, which submerged both these archdeacons, actually brought a bishop into the storm as a director of the forces of Churchmanship. In November 1847 a Mr. Gorham was presented to a living in the diocese of Exeter. Gorham was a Calvinist who held peculiar views about the sacramental grace of baptism, distinct from those of most Evangelicals, and strongly opposed to those of the Tractarians. The Bishop, Dr. Phillpotts, examined him at length on his views and decided not to institute him. The Ecclesiastical Court of Arches of the Province of Canterbury upheld the bishop, whereupon Gorham appealed to the Privy Council, in which seven civil judges sat on the case with the two Archbishops and the Bishop of London. Their judgment was delivered in March 1850, one lay judge and the Bishop of London dissenting. It declined to investigate the real opinions and teaching of Mr. Gorham, and pronounced a decision merely on certain extracts which the court had had before it; and on that basis acquitted Gorham of teaching anything that appeared to be, on a quite superficial construction of Anglican formularies, repugnant to the doctrine of the Church.

As the judgment was in flagrant conflict with the real facts, Bishop Phillpotts took a strong line and absolutely refused to institute Gorham, who was finally admitted to the benefice by authority of the Archbishop of Canterbury over Phillpotts' head. Phillpotts was entirely prepared to spend the rest of his life in gaol for contempt, rather than obey any mandate requiring him to institute Gorham. Although Pusey had from the first felt that the wiser course was to ignore Gorham's eccentricities and admit him, when Phillpotts asked him for assistance in defending the case before the Privy Council, Pusey threw himself into the task and continued to supply the bulk of the ammunition for the bishop's cannon. The bishop went down, indeed, but did so with colours flying defiance and with all his guns firing Pusey's double shot. Though the judgment acquitted Gorham, it made no direct breach in the teaching of the Church. The controversy proved in the end a moral victory for Churchmanship. But it was not so regarded at the time by that large section of Churchmen which was chiefly impressed by formal pronouncements and was unable to make allowance for circumstances. To them it appeared that the Church was in bondage to an alien civil power—which it was—and that its temporary impotence to resist the interference of civil force in its interior concerns fatally compromised its spiritual claims.

Keble was gravely shocked at the unsettling effect of the judgment on the minds of simple people: it seemed to imply that the highest legal authority did not care about the truth of baptismal grace. The Bishop of London introduced a bill into the House of Lords providing that the Privy Council court, while free to determine matters of fact, should be bound by the decision of the bishops on all questions of doctrine; but the bill was rejected. Agitation was conducted against the judgment by means of meetings, protests, petitions, literature. High Churchmen were once more reconciled to the Tractarian survivors, in denouncing the position of the Judicial Committee of the Privy Council as the final court of appeal in cases in which the Christian faith and discipline were involved. Pusey himself attempted in a book on the Royal Supremacy to meet the criticisms of the alarmists. Taking his stand on Christian antiquity, he showed how the civil power had at various times been allowed to summon Councils, nominate episcopal judges, enforce ecclesiastical decisions, and even require bishops to maintain ecclesiastical law. All this had been done by Christian Emperors acting as guardians of the Christian creeds and canons. What they had never done was to formulate doctrine, which was the matter that the Privy Council, while formally disclaiming such intention, had in fact, if only negatively and indirectly, attempted to undertake.

But the alarmists were not satisfied with anything short of the Roman position of the entire independence of ecclesiastical courts from secular control in questions of fact as much as in questions of faith. They assailed Pusey hotly for his moderation, and challenged the jurisdiction on which his very claim to officiate as a priest was based. Secessions began, as in 1845. Once more the High Church demanded a vehement anti-Roman policy, and once more Pusey discountenanced it, knowing that it would only precipitate the alarmists into the arms of Rome, and maintaining further that the negative principle of opposition to the Roman Church was no sure ground on which to establish religious unity. Besides, J.H.N. had written against Rome more daringly and vehemently than anyone; and whither had not that intolerance led him in the end ? But Manning resigned his preferments in the autumn, and in 1851 submitted to the Roman Church, whither Robert Wilberforce followed him after three years hesitation. Henry, another gifted Wilberforce brother, preceded him.

It was at this electric moment, in September 1850 that the Pope chose to constitute England an ecclesiastical province of the Roman Church, with an archbishop and twelve other diocesan bishops, instead of vicars-apostolic, to govern it. Immediately

an outcry was raised, comparable to that of 1845.
Pusey was again met with cold looks, where he was
not attacked with passionate invective. The bishops,
who by this time at least ought to have discovered
that Pusey and Keble alone could hold back from
Rome the waverers whom episcopal policy was
goading into secession, threw their weight into the
scale of popular denunciation. Only Bishop Phillpotts preserved an attitude of intelligence and
decency. Samuel Wilberforce, presumably thinking
it a poor advertisement for episcopal efficiency to be
losing two brothers to Popery, tried to make amends
by inhibiting Pusey, who was again almost overwhelmed with work and anxiety, from preaching in
the diocese. But this disgrace was averted from the
episcopate through the energetic representations of
J.K., Mr. Gladstone, and Mr. Justice Coleridge,
who severally told the bishop what they thought of
his action and staggered him by the force with
which they expressed it. A good consequence arose
from this sorry affair, since from 1851 Pusey and
Wilberforce were brought into relations of gradually
increasing respect and friendship. And as a direct
result of the Gorham judgment, the Convocations
were called out of abeyance in 1852, and allowed to
resume the free expression of the Church's voice,
which had been silenced since 1717. Thus good
again came out of evil.

Early in 1854 a new trouble began. Archdeacon

Denison, a stalwart and pugnacious Anglo-Catholic, was prosecuted for preaching the objective presence of the Body and Blood of Christ under the outward forms of the bread and wine in the Eucharist. A diocesan court at Bath, in which Archbishop Sumner for technical reasons presided, in place of the Bishop, condemned Denison. Since the ancient and Catholic belief in such an immaterial and spiritual, but 'real' and objective, Presence was a cardinal part of Tractarian and High Church faith, the decision caused the utmost dismay. Denison refused to retract and was deprived. On appeal, however, to the Court of Arches, the decision was reversed, though only on a technical point of law. The prosecutor took the matter to the Privy Council, which upheld the Court of Arches. The practical importance of this dispute was that it turned the minds of both Pusey and Keble to the treatment of Eucharistic theology. Neither of them intended to be driven out of the Church of England, and neither meant to be silenced. Pusey produced a characteristically learned collection of authorities on the subject, and Keble published an exquisite theological and devotional treatise on Eucharistical Adoration. In 1860, two years after the decision of the Privy Council, Pusey was able to render useful service to his dear friend, Bishop Forbes, of Brechin, in a similar attack made on his Eucharistic teaching in the Scottish Church.

The closing of this troubled period was marked by further private griefs for Pusey. Lady Emily, his elder brother's wife, who had been a true sister to him in all his sorrows, public and personal, died in 1854. His brother did not long survive this bereavement, dying in Pusey's house at Christ Church eight months later. Pusey's orphaned nephew and nieces came to live with him; but after a delightful six months they were removed from his care by the boy's guardians, who disapproved of Pusey's religious views. Pusey protested in deep distress, but vainly. In 1855 also Charles Marriott was struck down by paralysis, and, though he lived three years longer, it was as a helpless invalid.

Finally, in 1858, Pusey's beloved mother died, 'a pious, simple, and humble soul, who had served God and trusted in Jesus beyond the ordinary period of mortality,' as he himself described her. Writing to his younger brother, William Pusey, who was abroad at the time, Edward said that she had been waiting long at the gate of Paradise, always looking not to remain much longer; 'she has remained so much longer than we hoped, and now, in His mercy, she has entered into her rest.' In the presence of death Pusey maintained the true and cheerful faith of a Christian. But he practically never revisited the home of his childhood after his mother's death. No mother, she used to say, could have had a better son than God had given her; but he could not willingly bear to return to the scenes associated with those whom he had loved on earth in past years, or to indulge the sentiment of mourning. "Life," he said, "is too short to be spent on anything but the work which God has given us to do."

Chapter VII

THE TURN OF THE TIDE

PUSEY WAS JUST AS OLD as the nineteenth century, having been born in 1800, so that as the 'fifties grew on he himself was now passing middle age. But neither his capacity for hard work nor his opportunities for undertaking it diminished. On the contrary, new openings developed which he felt it his duty to employ. And, strangely enough, it was in Oxford, where his work had begun and where his overthrow had been most complete, that his rehabilitation in general esteem also started; and it came about through a process of events which he had done his utmost to prevent. History, though on paper it is not infrequently written with the dullest of dull pens, is nevertheless in fact and substance often composed by a Mind to which irony and epigram are no strangers.

The reign of the Tories over the university had now at last come to an end, and the Younger Liberals were busily engaged in refashioning their *Alma Mater* as a Liberal Lady. The older Liberals had for the most part transferred the aristocratic temper of political Whigs to the academic sphere; they were either intellectual purists or moral libertarians; they patronized Dissenters in order to annoy High Churchmen, but their minds worked in thoroughly traditional grooves. The younger school had been trained by Dr. Arnold in very different principles. It was much more independent and searching in its criticism, and wore with distinction a white robe of moral endeavour that no humour could variegate. Yet its members were far more human than their predecessors in their interests and sympathies, and were, like Pusey, keen supporters of the social and moral advancement of the depressed classes. But their perception of the crying need for change in many aspects of the national life was accompanied by a corresponding disregard for the providential ordering of the past; they tended to think that everything which was decently old was indecently narrow, if not noisomely defunct. And they belonged to that generation which believed with all its heart in the omnipotence of utilitarian politics; to make men moral by Act of Parliament was to them not a joke but a pious crusade.

This temper made them great, if somewhat inconsiderate, reformers, and in 1850 they got their chance to reform the University of Oxford. The Government appointed a Commission to inquire into the state of the university, consisting of persons notoriously Liberal in politics and mainly Latitudinarian in religion; of which Tait, now Dean of Carlisle, was one of the foremost members, and Stanley (afterwards Dean of Westminster) was the secretary. Oxford, whether Tory or Tractarian, was no whit less scandalized for the fact that it was impotent to resist; but it resisted stoutly all the same. In 1852 the Commission reported, advocating sweeping reforms of the old system alike in finance, government, and educational methods; but before further action was taken a chance was given to the university to express its criticisms, and in this work Pusey played a very prominent part.

His conception of education was perfectly definite. Looking to the end and object of the whole matter rather than to the means by which that object can be best achieved, he asserted that the problem and special work of a university was neither scientific discovery, nor philosophical speculation, nor learned research, even in such a subject as theology; "but to form minds religiously, morally, intellectually, which shall discharge aright whatever duties God in His providence shall appoint to them." In fact, he was thinking less of the particular functions of modern universities than of the whole duty of man, and wanted to maintain the ideal, now no longer practicable, of combining into a single system of higher education every type of educational influence which ought ideally to be brought to bear in their earlier years on the more intelligent members of a Christian society. His conception was magnificent but it was not practical politics. His criticisms of certain parts of the Report, his dislike of the specialization which it would inevitably promote, and his objection against the transference of emphasis from discipline to mere knowledge, and from religion to mere cleverness, represent the dignified and far from illiberal protestation of a system of culture in process of dissolution, addressed to the elements which were dissolving its existence.

The strange sight was seen, and noted with some disconcertment by J.K., of Dr. Pusey once more in alliance with the Heads of Houses who had persecuted him for so long. But the great days of '33 were not to be repeated. Gladstone, now a power in the Government, had taken up the University question with immense thoroughness, and to Pusey's sorrow threw all his influence on the side of reformation. Parliament passed an Act in 1854, under which an Executive Commission was appointed to carry out, not indeed all that the earlier Commission had recommended, but enough to establish the transformation of a seventeenth-century Oxford into a very dissimilar institution. Among many other reforms of principle and of detail, religious restrictions were abolished for undergraduates; a similar measure affecting University and College teachers and members of the Convocation, which had the ultimate legislative power in the university, was carried through, again by the Tractarian Gladstone, in 1871. The University thus became the handmaid of civil society, and no longer that of the Church; and except in its Theological Faculty ministered thenceforward to religious learning, for the sake of which it had mainly come into existence, only indirectly, in so far as all true learning involves knowledge of God for those who understand religious truth.

Pusey regretted this fundamental change with his whole soul, and fought it as long as it could be fought. But he was a truly humble man, entirely free from the spirit of antagonism. Consequently, when everything was settled in a way of which he disapproved, he was so far from retiring into a spiritual sulk that he again became among the foremost, no longer in opposing, but in accepting and working the novel constitution. When the new Hebdomadal Council met in October 1854, to carry on the government of the university, Pusey was among its members, and he retained his place at every election until infirmity compelled him to withdraw in 1878. To the astonishment of certain of his old opponents, he immediately made his mark as an admirable man of business. On his own part, he was delighted to find that this new association with other leading men, which, to the extent of attendance at Council and committees, brought him out of the strict seclusion of fifteen years, led to reconciliations with some long-lost friends and to the formation of fresh sentiments of regard towards many who differed altogether from him in their religious and academic views.

But the work caused serious in-roads on his time. Council was meeting, in 1855, for three afternoons a week, not to mention various committees. Its business increased his already immense correspondence, conducted with friends and strangers, clergy and politicians, nuns and undergraduates, and almost every other category of human beings, on every sort of subject bearing on religion. A modern Dean of Christ Church once wrote a hymn tune, afterwards published in a well-known collection of hymnody, during a particularly boring meeting of the Hebdomadal Council. Pusey made a habit of taking with him to its meetings bundles of letters or proof-sheets, and employed the valuable leisure that accrued during unprofitable speech-making by addressing spiritual advice to his numerous penitents or in correcting the proofs of his next publication.

He was indefatigable as professor. All his work was prepared with the most elaborate care, whether it were Council business or a course of lectures or a sermon for the University pulpit. It is an entire mistake to suppose that his time was mainly occupied with ecclesiastical controversy. He raised the estimation of his Hebrew chair to a high pitch of repute, and remained, as he had begun, a scholar of European distinction. He was over sixty when he mastered a new Oriental language, Ethiopic. He not only lectured, and sometimes made his lectures the substance of a massive book, as that on the

Prophet Daniel, published in 1864; he also formed discussion circles, attended by undergraduate pupils and bachelors of arts, to meet at his own house for the consideration of particular problems of Old Testament criticism. There were other giants of industry in Oxford in the middle of last century, but nobody surpassed the delicate Professor Pusey in unremitting labour.

Since he had reverted from his earlier views on Biblical inspiration to what would now be called a form of fundamentalism, it is important to observe what was Pusey's attitude towards natural science. Scholar though he was, he was no classical die-hard, despising everything in education that was not based on literature. One of the chief reasons why he had always so delighted in Keble's *Christian Year* was because 'dear J.K. so listened to Nature and interpreted it to us.' He had at different times shown a practical desire to assist biological studies in the university, and supported their advancement by his vote and influence in Council at a critical moment in 1855. Scientists of distinction were numbered among his friends. In his later years he was unable, from pressure of work, to follow every movement in the scientific world, but he continued as before to read and advise on books which created concern to the faith of his correspondents. Darwin's *Descent of Man* distressed him, because he thought it implied that the human mind and soul were derived without any evolutionary gap from the pithecoids. But so long as it was agreed that man's personality was a direct divine creation, he could bear to contemplate, albeit with a sceptical shudder, the possibility of his physical descent from ape-like ancestors.

He resolutely declined to be afraid of science, or to admit for a moment that it was necessarily or permanently in opposition to theology. He preached on Christian faith in 1855. "Faith, from first to last, is the gift of God to the soul which will receive it. God prepares the soul, with its will, not without it, to receive the faith. God stills the soul, that it may listen to the faith; God flashes conviction into the soul, that it may see the truth of the faith; in those who through His grace persevere to the end, God seals up the faith in the soul, that it may keep the faith which it has received." Mere intellect cannot command the attainment of conviction, nor ignorance preclude it. On the other hand: "Reason, healed, restored, guided, enlightened, by the Spirit of God, has a power of vision above nature." The settlement of the clash which seemed to shake the educated world was, as he pointed out in a great address to the Church Congress in 1865, to be found in the fact that faith and science have quite distinct spheres, which are not commensurate. "Science relates to causes and effects, the laws by which God upholds His material creation, or its past history. Faith relates to God, His Revelation, His Word"; is, in fact, a "God-given habit of mind," by means of which the conclusions of natural experience are reviewed and interpreted in a Christian philosophy of life. Hence, "What really lies outside the peasant's faith, cannot really touch the faith of any, however intellectual." "This then is our attitude toward any researches of any science; entire fearlessness as to the issue; awaiting that issue, undisturbed, whenever it shall unfold itself." It was a wise and independent line for the head and front of the Tractarians to take in 1865.

But Pusey was always independent. He had recently differed from most of his own supporters in a more domestic controversy. In 1855 the famous Benjamin Jowett had been appointed Regius Professor of Greek. This professorship was very poorly paid, and successive attempts were made to have the endowment increased. Unfortunately the professor had dabbled somewhat disastrously in theology in such a manner as to raise serious doubts about his faith in the Atonement and the Person of Christ; and the increase of his salary was vehemently opposed, on the ground that such action would be taken to signify indifference to religious faith, public adherence to which was then still required of teachers in the university, though not of their pupils. The proposal was from the first a personal affair, and Pusey was necessarily drawn into the dispute.

Pusey and Keble both made efforts to secure a solution, by which the professor should be paid, while his theology was disowned. In 1860 Pusey persuaded Council to accept a plan by which no favour should be manifested to Jowett personally, but two badly paid Regius professorships should be simultaneously endowed as an act of academic justice, Jowett's being one. The Government consented to the scheme, but next year, in spite of Pusey's advocacy, a combination of the older and orthodox Liberals with the Churchly party defeated it in the Convocation. H. P. Liddon, on whom Pusey now chiefly depended to keep him in touch with the younger High Churchmen, voted against his leader, being duly rebuked therefor by J.K.; and Pusey experienced the strange happiness of being publicly thanked by Stanley for his efforts. A fresh attempt made by Pusey was again defeated in 1864, but a settlement was reached in 1865 by Christ Church providing the necessary funds for endowing the Greek professorship from College revenues.

Pusey's consistent advocacy of economic justice to a religious opponent was all the more creditable since Jowett had become involved in a still more serious affair than his previous theological escapade. Jowett strongly resented the feel of orthodox shackles on his too sensitive organs of thought; being "determined not to submit to this abominable system of terrorism"—by which he meant the Oxford orthodoxy which had once crushed the Tractarians and now threatened to press on the Younger Liberals— he took an active part in the production of the provocative *Essays and Reviews*, which appeared in 1860. This publication, which had been deprecated beforehand as inopportune by Stanley, and was condemned even by Tait, now Bishop of London, made a tremendous row, the black unorthodoxy of the less important contributors casting a demonic halo round the heads of the comparatively inoffensive Jowett and the quite innocuous Frederick Temple, who was later, like Tait, to become Archbishop of Canterbury.

Pusey wrote to the press to say that the book contained little which had not been familiar for thirty years to students who followed the course of German rationalism; but the public panic could not be allayed. Twenty-four bishops, including Tait—to the wrath of his contemporary Liberals—and Hampden, the old bugbear of the early Tractarians, issued a public letter condemning the tendencies of the work, though without expressly naming it, and expressing surprise at its authors' claim to be honest Anglicans. Shortly afterwards, in the summer of 1861, prosecutions were instituted against two of the authors. The Court of Arches condemned them, and they promptly appealed to the Privy Council, which in 1864, on much the same grounds as in the Gorham case, reversed the condemnation, alleging that the essays contained no express contradiction in set terms of any authorized formulary of the Church. In effect the Privy Council once more declined to investigate the doctrinal issue seriously, whitewashed the accused by placing an unjustifiably hopeful interpretation on their statements, and by this double depreciation of theology tended to make it appear that clergy of the Church of England could hold infidel opinions without risking the forfeiture of their claim to act as her accredited teachers or the guides of Christian souls.

Pusey and Wilberforce were wholly reconciled by their common opposition to this legal farce. High and Low Church joined forces in protest, an event which led Tait to record in his diary the conviction that it was part of his own vocation to prevent the coalescence of High and Low Church against the spread of Broad Church teaching—a singular confession of fostering disunion in the Church to be made by one of its most influential bishops. Both archbishops proclaimed their belief in the doctrines which had been impugned by the essayists; 137,000 laymen signed an address of thanks to them for doing so. At the instance of Wilberforce a declaration was drawn up, in which Pusey had a considerable part, declaring adherence to the two beliefs in the inspiration of the canonical Scriptures and the everlasting reprobation of the impenitent: eleven thousand clergymen signed it. Finally, both

Houses of the Convocation of Canterbury solemnly condemned the whole volume of *Essays and Reviews*, an action which was quite unfair, at least to Temple.

These somewhat tumultuous judgments were hasty and unfortunate. Involved questions of Biblical criticism could not be satisfactorily settled thus, in the heat of passion and to some extent by mere clamour. But at any rate the dispute completed the dethronement of the Judicial Committee of the Privy Council from any position of moral authority which it might ever have held as a court of ecclesiastical appeal, though Churchmen were unable to agree on a satisfactory substitute.

It is interesting to notice what was Pusey's own attitude towards the whole question of ecclesiastical prosecutions, and to observe his reasons for supporting a line of action that is sometimes thought to savour of intolerance. All his life had been spent in the defence of revelation; he perceived, with greater clearness than many of his contemporaries, that the Church was an association with certain definite principles to maintain; there might be room for differences of opinion about the interpretation to be put on them, but about the facts which form the basis of the Christian solution of the problems of humanity no doubt can be entertained without dissolving the Christian message and destroying the Christian life. There must accordingly be some limit set, not to the freedom of speculation, but to the recognition and admission of speculative thinkers to the Christian ministry of teaching.

All his life Pusey had also conscientiously tried to act under obedience. He was often forced to ignore the bishops, but only because the bishops flagrantly ignored the express formularies of the Church, which it was Pusey's mission to expound and defend. He justified himself at every step by the teaching of the Prayer Book and Articles, the Creeds and the Bible, the Anglican theological tradition and the ancient Fathers to whom that tradition appealed. To determine the sense of theological tradition is a matter for critical research, and the conclusion, when reached, is not of necessity binding on a later generation. But to discover the limits of interpretation which the Church has expressly defined, and to which every clergyman was in individual loyalty bound by his oaths and declarations, was a matter for legal enquiry. Pusey therefore consistently approved of ecclesiastical prosecution about doctrinal questions, not because he wished to persecute opponents, but simply because it was the only practical method of ascertaining and establishing authoritatively the facts of what the Church, to which he owed obedience, really taught. He was positively anxious to be prosecuted himself, in order to fulfil that purpose; on at least three separate occasions he trailed his coat before bishops, university, Church courts, and the Protestant society called the Church Association, begging them in vain to prosecute him. He claimed no right to remain in the Church of England if it was honestly established that he was not truly loyal to her teaching. Had he been condemned, he would without hesitation have resigned his position and betaken himself, not to Rome, but to Scotland or elsewhere. Whether every prosecution with which he was connected was wisely conceived, is one question, and open to serious doubt; that the Church was rendered absurd, and in a measure impotent by the policy of the Privy Council, in practically depriving her of all rational process of legal enquiry, is another matter, and beyond dispute.

Mention has been made of Liddon. By 1864 he was becoming Pusey's chief and most active lieutenant. In that year Pusey invited him to a meeting of leaders with the humorous observation: "I hope you will be there; you are quite old enough to be an Arch-conspirator." Liddon was more Tractarian than the Tractarians in all but the employment of a biting irony, a weapon which they had been too gentle to allow themselves; he regarded the utterances of Pusey as next in importance after Holy Scripture, and as the foremost preacher of his age enjoyed ample opportunity of spreading his master's faith. It was well for the cause that it had found this younger captain, who was still only thirty-five in 1864. Pusey was now sixty-four, and J.K. was eight years older.

Since shortly after his secession, in 1845, Newman had never seen either Pusey or Keble, though letters had passed between them. In the summer of 1865 Keble was anxious for Newman to pay him a visit. Newman had fixed a day, when he heard accidentally that Pusey was going to Hursley on the same date. He could not face such a reunion charged with the memories of old love stronger than heart-break; so he wrote to say that he would stay with friends in the Isle of Wight, and come over to Hursley some day later to see Keble. On 12th September he got into the train at Birmingham to carry out this plan.

Next morning, when Keble was standing at his front door in conversation with a friend, an elderly gentleman walked up, who obviously did not know him. Keble asked him his name. The stranger, still unable to recognize J.K. with certainty, presented his card in silence. It was dear J.H.N. He had decided that it was mere cowardice to shirk the meeting, slept at Southampton, and arrived at Hursley in the forenoon, unannounced, unexpected. Mrs. Keble was ill. "Pusey is in the house," whispered J.K.; he led Newman into the study, embraced him with tender affection, and went out again to prepare Pusey and send him in to Newman. The whole incident was savage evidence of the passage of years. But the happiness of the three old

gentlemen was nearly complete. They dined together without any fourth party, a thing they had
apparently never done before in old times; they
talked theology—Newman, who reports the matter,
here sounds faintly reserved; they discussed politics
subject to fewer reservations; Keble made a
humorous aside, of which the manner impressed
itself more deeply on Newman's memory than the
matter; then Pusey went off to say Evensong in the
Parish Church, and the other two strolled, Keble
conversing "with more than his old tone of intimacy,
as if we had never been parted." So the time for
departure came, and a wonderful day ended. The
local press got wind of the event, and stated that
Pusey and Newman had been 'reconciled after
twenty years.' Pusey was as nearly infuriated as a
mild and disciplined character could be. "The deep
love between us, which now dates back for above
forty years, has never been in the least over-
shadowed." And that was final.

In the following March dear J.K., who was staying at Bournemouth for the sake of his wife's health,
had a paralytic stroke and died. No dignity in the
English Church had ever been conferred on him.
But he had no need either of buttons crawling up
his legs or of superfluous laces in his hat to give him
dignity. The highest honour that he could desire
was for Dr. Pusey to love him. He was not even in his
grave before his friends had definitely decided to

build a new College in Oxford to be called by his name. Nor do they seem to have felt any misgiving about the cost : too many Oxford men owed their soul to J.K. for the money to concern them. Nevertheless, on the day of the funeral Pusey was almost overcome. "I never saw Dr. Pusey so broken as to-day," wrote Liddon in his diary; "he seemed to feel quite terribly the weight of responsibility which had devolved on him." The tide had indeed turned in Church affairs, and at the Church Congress of 1865 Pusey's appearance had been received with tumultuous cheering. But dearest J.K. was gone, to whom he had written on Keble's last birthday "to express my thankfulness for the many and great mercies which God gave us through giving you to us to-day," and on whose quiet strength and counsel he had hoped to be able to rely "for years to come." For the first time of his life Pusey found himself alone in his own generation.

Chapter VIII

A FATHER IN ISRAEL

ONE OF THE EARLIEST RESULTS of the renewed
devotion aroused among the laity by the Oxford
Movement, and by the study of Christian antiquity
which it encouraged, was a desire, which sprang up
independently in several quarters, for a life of dedication under religious vows. In 1839 both Pusey and
Newman were considering the idea of establishing a
community of Sisters of Charity, and during 1840
considerable correspondence passed with Dr. Hook
at Leeds on the subject. Hook was sympathetic, and
his sister, who was however tied for the time being
by family obligations, felt strongly drawn towards
the religious life. Newman stressed the fact that if an
outlet were not made for the fulfilment of such
vocations in the Church of England, people who felt
the call would go to the Church of Rome to find
their opportunity. Pusey and Hook enlarged on the
practical value of the scheme, if it could be brought
into operation; the heathen in the slums of the great
cities knew no more about the Gospel than did the
inhabitants of Thibet, and were untouched by
ordinary parish organization; but they could be
reached and taught by Sisters whose whole existence
was consecrated to their special service and instruction.

Community life for men was also under discussion. Newman's group at Littlemore lived under
rule from 1842, and might have developed into an
order in course of time and experience. The clergy
at St. Saviour's, Leeds, were from the first designed
to live a collegiate, though not a monastic, life.
Other tentative beginnings were tried elsewhere.
But they were brought to nothing by the growing
tendency of their members Romeward, which
culminated in the secessions of 1845. Small experiments continued to be made, but nothing permanent
was achieved till 1866, when the Society of St.
John the Evangelist was established at Cowley,
close to Oxford, by Father Benson, a senior member
of Christ Church. It was far otherwise with the
women. Though nothing immediate came out of
the negotiations with Hook, Pusey was in direct
touch with two ladies who had decided to dedicate
themselves to the religious life. One of these was his
own eldest child, Lucy, who had recognized her
vocation, and determined to follow it, at the age of
twelve. Her mother had made a special emphasis
of Newman's influence in the child's education; her
own character and the exceptional sympathy
between her and her father gave this influence its
practical direction. Pusey looked forward with the
deepest joy and thankfulness to her making her
profession as a Sister. But, as has been said, she died
before she was fifteen. Pusey's charge to her on her

death-bed was to pray, within the veil, 'for those
institutions to which she had herself hoped to
belong.'

The other lady was a Miss Hughes, who was also
a disciple, though from afar, of Newman. Acting
under Pusey's counsel she had reached the point of
wishing to take a private vow of holy celibacy, since
as yet no Sisterhood existed for her to join; and on
the same day on which Lucy received her first
Communion, at St. Mary's, in 1841, Miss Hughes
was present, too, and made her vow. But one vow
does not make a religious community. A very great
deal of preparation was first required. Pusey was
well aware of the spiritual dangers attending the re-
establishment of a mode of life which no direct
tradition existed to regulate and for which there was
no Anglican precedent in the past three hundred
years. Enthusiasm without discipline was not
enough to keep the new movement out of the pitfalls
of fanaticism and ascetic indiscretion. The first
necessity was therefore the formation of a wise rule.
Pusey himself paid a long visit to Ireland in 1841 to
make enquiries about the methods employed in
Roman convents. He was very kindly received by
the Roman authorities, but seems to have acquired
more distaste for the exaggerated devotion paid to
the Blessed Virgin than useful information about
community life. In the same summer, however, Miss
Hughes was despatched to Normandy with a

married clergyman and his wife to gather what knowledge she could about French Sisterhoods, and brought back full details of some of their rules, both published and unpublished. These provided sufficient information to form the basis of the first rule for Anglican Sisters, which was afterwards modified in the light of practical experience.

There ensued further delay, partly due to the troubles of the time and the phrenetic anti-Popery that swept over the English Church. Pusey, living as always for the day and unconcerned for futurity except to lay strong and deep foundations, recognized the providential value of inaction; it would serve to discipline and ripen the characters of the postulants. The first definite step was taken in London by a group of prominent laymen, on the very day of Lucy Pusey's funeral in 1844. They wrote to Pusey, stating that they had decided to establish and maintain a house for Sisters, and asking his advice in the all-important matter of a Superior for the proposed community. The work of the Sisters was to include visiting the poor and sick in their homes, and the inmates of hospitals, workhouses, and prisons; feeding, clothing, and teaching destitute children; and assisting in the burial of the dead. The question of a Superior had to be left for later consideration, but Pusey threw himself into the task of drawing up a rule and framing a scheme of devotions; and shortly after

Easter 1845 the first Sisters were established at Park Village West, in London. The great experiment was started with eight Sisters, Pusey being their spiritual superintendent. They lived and prayed in great simplicity, ministering to the roughest class, and teaching in a Ragged School the children who were too neglected to be admitted elsewhere to the benefits of education. Prejudice was soon lived down, and before long they had won the hearts of the people.

Further experiments followed, usually in connexion with some parish where the sympathies were Tractarian, such as those of St. Thomas, Oxford (1847), Wantage (1848), All Saints, Margaret Street (1851), Clewer (1852), and East Grinstead (1855); but for these Pusey had a less direct responsibility. At the end of three years the rule of the Park Village Sisterhood was submitted to the Bishop of London, and approved by him; the revival was beginning to pass out of the stage of pure experiment. Pusey was frequently asked to advise on the foundation of fresh communities, but with notable insight he discountenanced the indefinite multiplication of small Sisterhoods in separate parishes. Sisters, and, above all, Superiors, had to be trained, and for that purpose it was infinitely wiser to send postulants to one of the established communities. But he was concerned in two other foundations. In 1849 the Society of the Holy and Undivided Trinity was started at Oxford under Miss Hughes, who survived to rule over her convent until 1912. And a year earlier a work was begun at Devonport with which Pusey was to maintain the most intimate association until his death.

An appeal had been made by Bishop Phillpotts, of Exeter, for churches and schools, in order to relieve the spiritual and moral destitution of the great seaport in his diocese. Miss Sellon, the strong-minded daughter of a naval officer, volunteered to teach, and on Pusey's recommendation was sent with a friend to one of the new parishes which were being formed at Devonport, where she displayed remarkable capacity in organizing schools of extremely varied types both for boys and for girls. She was rapidly led to extend her activities; a home was started for sailors' orphans, and interest was taken in female passengers on the emigrant ships; the shortage of clergy made it necessary for her to undertake the preparation of candidates for baptism and confirmation. Such a vast range of work called as urgently for close organization as did the workers' spiritual enthusiasm for disciplined control. Pusey went down on a visit of inspection and found the regeneration of the district already effected to be almost incredible, but that the obvious need for the consolidation and development of the work was for it to be put on a community basis. Before the year ended the bishop came to Devonport, saw what was happening, and gave his hearty sanction to the plan of forming a religious community, himself becoming its visitor.

Protestant fanaticism ran high in Plymouth at that period. The incumbent of one of the parishes in which the Sisters laboured was accused to the bishop of such heinous offences as wearing a surplice during the sermon and employing velvet bags in which to collect the alms. On the bishop's dismissal of the objections raised against these malpractices, the attack was switched over to the Sisters, against whom, and against Pusey, a number of devotional enormities were alleged, in particular that Pusey celebrated Holy Communion in the Sisters' oratory, which was not licensed by the bishop for that purpose. Dr. Phillpotts was a rabid disciplinarian. He promptly ordered an enquiry, and came down in person, in February 1849, to conduct it. The charge of celebrating unlawfully in an unlicensed building was disproved; the bishop lauded Pusey to the skies, and said the Sisters were honoured to have him for their friend. As for the Sisters themselves, he had come to the enquiry with a feeling of veneration for Miss Sellon's work and character: he went away with a feeling that he could not express —of unmixed admiration and reverence. This was a handsome testimonial to Puseyism at a time when most of the bishops were either assigning its origin or consigning its future to the devil. Perhaps his admiration was in part the result of finding in Miss Sellon a sister autocrat; her large conception of the holy obedience due to a Superior caused considerable difficulties; but his judgment was at any rate a triumph for the society. This triumph was accentuated four months later, when cholera broke out with terrible virulence in Devonport and the Sisters claimed, and exercised to the full, the right of ministering to the sick and dying in the epidemic. So through mingled heroism and persecution this Sisterhood won an established position with exceptional rapidity.

In 1854 the Park Village Sisterhood came to the end of its independent existence. The Superior and other Sisters joined Florence Nightingale's band of nurses in the Crimea; the surviving members of the community were united to the Devonport Sisterhood. In 1861 the united society started a convalescent home at Ascot for the benefit of the sick poor of whom their London work brought them knowledge, and in 1877 the Devonport orphanage, after an intervening migration to London, finally came to rest at Ascot Priory also. For nearly thirty years, from 1855 onwards, Pusey's enterprise caused the Sisters to maintain a printing-press, to which the older and more intelligent orphans were drafted. This course was not dictated by ideas of feminism. Pusey's common sense observed that one of the main causes which induced women to sell themselves into prostitution was simply want of money. Accordingly, though he valued the work of penitentiaries for the rescue of girls who had already fallen, he perceived that much the most important remedy lay in enabling young women to earn a respectable living at respectable wages. So he had them trained as compositors. "Englishmen," he said, "have a monomania about penitentiaries"; they will do anything in order to pluck a few unhappy and half-stifled beings out of the black, muddied, filthy stream, but are entirely apathetic about stopping the supply of fresh misery with which the stream is being perpetually renewed. "I would not, then, discourage penitentiaries—but for one penitentiary, I should be glad to have ten abodes for training destitute poor female children." It is to be feared, however, that after eighty years there are still many good Christians who are anxious, in all innocence, to keep women out of jobs, unless they are unpaid.

In 1864, after a breakdown from overwork, Pusey found in Ascot a retreat which admirably suited his delicate health. He often returned there to recuperate, and formed the habit of spending every Long Vacation in a small house near the Hospital, among the pine woods. Two of the greatest joys of his later years were the presentation to the Hospital of a considerable sum of money from private friends as a token of personal affection for himself, and the consent of the Princess of Wales, Alexandra, to become its patroness. This work lay all the nearer to his heart because it was being done for the orphan and the sick and those least capable of fighting their own battles. It was relaxation to him to be among them, and watch the happiness which Ascot brought to their faces; and at Ascot, among them, he died.

During 1865 practical consideration was being given to another plan, to found a religious community for men. Five years earlier Pusey had, through Miss Sellon, had some dealings with the brilliant and erratic Father Ignatius, who about that time assumed the Benedictine habit; Pusey encouraged his monastic purpose, while maintaining a wholesome distrust of his judgment. But the new venture was of a different character, with the Rev. R. M. Benson, a saintly master of the spiritual life, for its moving spirit, and a band of wise and experienced advisers, including Pusey himself, Keble, the Bishop of Brechin, Liddon, and the Hon. C. L. Wood (since better known as Lord Halifax), as its supporters. Benson was a Student of Christ Church and Vicar of Cowley, being thus in close contact with Pusey. Consultations had already been some time in progress, when an American priest, Mr. Grafton, later Bishop of Fond du Lac, sailed from Boston to Liverpool, travelled straight to Oxford and made his confession to Pusey, heard from him of the steps which had been taken, and threw in his lot with the movement.

His letters cast an interesting light on the foundation. 'God is most marvellously working in this portion of His Church. By a series of wonderful providences men are being drawn to a religious life, and are being drawn together. It is the most awful and solemn of anything I ever knew. . . If God will, very quietly indeed in the autumn some persons will get together and the work be begun. Some of England's saintliest men will direct by their counsel the work, and some of them will be in it. . . . As soon as we can, we will meet at a place near Oxford, Mr. Benson's parish, and commence living by rule and receiving instruction in the spiritual life and rules of a community.' In this quiet and solid fashion Father Benson and his companions, working with Pusey's approbation and assistance, brought into existence in 1866 the Society of St. John the Evangelist. The extent of Pusey's influence may be estimated by the fact that Father Benson retained for him the greatest veneration, and during the last two years of Pusey's life was to be found, whenever possible, attending Pusey's university lectures on the Hebrew Bible. It is an uncommon thing for university lectures to be both delivered and attended by saints.

The important part which Pusey played in the restoration of religious communities in the English

Church emphasizes an aspect of his life-work which may easily be overlooked. He was great in many fields; as theologian, particularly, though by no means solely, in the department of patristic erudition; as serious controversialist in defence of Church principles; as leader and guide in profoundly important matters of Church policy. But his work as pastoral counsellor, discreet and learned in the knowledge and direction of the spiritual life, ranks not a bit behind the rest; and its value stands pre-eminent by reason of the fact that it was necessarily experimental to a great extent. The science of the spiritual life had been almost entirely neglected in the English Church for two centuries. Experience had to be formed afresh and knowledge acquired from such sources as were available. That is the reason why, as early as 1844, Pusey engaged in translating foreign Roman manuals of devotion and adapting them for use by Anglican loyalists. Such compilations were the best that could be got, and in default of any other supply the best Roman books, like the best Roman rules for religious communities, had to be transplanted. From time to time popular attacks were made on Pusey for this practice; but the attacks were in the circumstances totally unreasonable. As practical experience of such matters was acquired, the need for foreign adaptations gradually lessened; but he would be a rash man even to-day who could seriously assert that English Churchmen have nothing left to learn from their fellow-Catholics abroad.

In 1856 Pusey's house was employed for one of the first retreats for clergy held in the course of the Anglican revival. But his greatest work as a practical pastor of souls lay in his exercise of the ministry of penance. It has been claimed that Pusey probably heard more confessions than any other priest in the Church of England, though he never urged people to confession; the penitents presented themselves spontaneously. He was a practical confessor, and went straight to the point. At the same time he was infinitely patient with people who had real difficulties. He was once engaged in an unexpectedly long interview with an undergraduate when the servant tapped at the door and said: "The fly is here, sir, to take you to the station." Pusey simply replied: "Oh, find me another train, will you?" On another occasion he spent twenty-two hours at a stretch, praying beside a death-bed in the protracted agony of the patient. His advice was sensible; he strongly deprecated, in others, excessive rigour in fasting or neglect of proper sleep, and he discouraged all undue reliance on emotion. He was ruthless in exposing conceit and class-consciousness; but "tender and pitiful to the sinner who was repentant, humble, and submissive." Many others followed in his path, but Pusey did more than any one to blaze the trail.

Another cause which had engaged his warm

interest from an early period was that of the education of ordinands, particularly of poor men whose parents could not afford to send them to the university through the ordinary college channels. He was concerned with various abortive schemes, from 1833 onwards, for training ordinands at cathedral centres or in hostels at Oxford. One of his strong grounds for opposing the secularization of Oxford teaching was that it took away from the Church the opportunity of training ordinands as well as laymen. The need later came to be met by the establishment of theological colleges, and by the foundation of the Honour School of Theology, in 1868, in which Pusey took an active part. But he was still anxious to secure an opportunity for members of the Church of England to receive a general university education in an atmosphere of Churchmanship. His chance came when the question of a memorial to Keble was raised.

It was decided from the first instant that the memorial should take the form of an Anglican college at Oxford. Munificent benefactions poured in, and Pusey watched every step in the foundation with anxious care. The first stone was laid by the Archbishop of Canterbury in 1868; the first undergraduates came into residence three years later. The new institution offered a first-class academic training to Churchmen of narrow means; it was to be a school of faith, a school of simplicity, where men could be trained to be good soldiers of Jesus Christ in whatever vocation they might be called to fulfil. Keble College was to stand as an active and positive protest against secularism and against luxury, the two greatest enemies in Pusey's outlook. The chapel was opened in 1876, on Keble's birthday, when Pusey preached a magnificent sermon on 'Blessed are the Meek.' How meek was Moses; how meek was David; how meek was dear John Keble. He had shrunk from publishing *The Christian Year*. He had been injured and reviled, yet he reviled not again. He talked no controversy, but he lived. The Passion of his Lord, Whom he loved, was his book, his life; he lived, because Christ lived in him. It was a great example for the school of faith, the school of simplicity, to follow.

And at last Pusey began to be surrounded in Oxford by senior men whom he trusted and who trusted him. Liddon was elected Ireland Professor in 1870. About the same time the cathedral chapter was enriched with three professors of great distinction who had strong Tractarian sympathies. Bright became Regius Professor of Ecclesiastical History in 1869; J. B. Mozley, one of the students who had lived in Pusey's house in 1836, was appointed by Mr. Gladstone to be Regius Professor of Divinity in 1871; and Edward King, one of the two foremost of the second generation of Tractarian saints, the beloved Principal of Cuddesdon and later the no less beloved Bishop of Lincoln, was nominated by the same Prime Minister as Regius Professor of Pastoral Theology in 1873. After half of a long lifetime blackened with academic storms, Pusey could see streamers of gold in the sunset.

Chapter IX

THE BRIDGE-BUILDER

PUSEY WAS AN INCORRIGIBLE DEVOTEE of religious unity. He welcomed every possible opportunity for co-operation with the Evangelicals, nor was his ardour damped by the fewness of the opportunities which the Evangelicals permitted him to enjoy. He continued to love them, for the same reason as had first attracted him towards them, that they loved our Lord, with devotion though not always with knowledge. On similar grounds he refused to speak ill of Romanists; they served the same Master, even if, sometimes, with better discipline than discrimination. He loved and longed for peace, and was the mildest controversialist that ever laid an adversary low with pen and ink.

In 1834 he wrote that the Dissenters "have taken up the ground which the Church in the days of her supineness left waste. . . . I hope yet some means may be devised by which the Wesleyans at least may be reunited to the Church." In 1840 he consulted his bishop, who, in turn, consulted Canterbury, about a plan for banding together a group of intercessors to pray for unity; the prelates thought it rather rash to exceed the measure of such prayers prescribed in the liturgical services, even though the form of the proposed devotions was taken from the

Prayer Book; nevertheless, the plan was adopted in a very small and private way, and led in 1845 to the issue by Pusey, Keble, and Marriott of prayers for unity, for the conversion of sinners, and for the advancement of the faithful, intended for daily use at regular hours. Again in 1840 he enquires: "What should hinder communion from being restored with the Orthodox Greek Church?" There was as yet no German Old Catholic Church in existence, but it is extremely interesting to find Pusey, in 1842, in correspondence with Döllinger, destined to become the tragic hero of 1870. "I have read almost all your works," wrote Döllinger, and, though he could not but regret some passages, "there is *far more* in them with which I can entirely agree, nay—what seemed to be written out of my own soul." He 'devoured' the Tractarian publications.

When Newman seceded, Pusey thought that "as each, by God's grace, grows in holiness, each Church will recognize, more and more, the presence of God's Holy Spirit in the other; and what now hinders the union of the Western Church will fall off." The hotter the conflict grew with unbelief, the closer did he expect those Christian bodies would be drawn together which maintained the substance of the common faith in the common creeds. He hoped that if another General Council could be summoned, the decrees by which the Roman Church was formally bound might be explained in a sense which would make them possible of acceptance by Anglicans. But he was somewhat checked by the appearance of Newman's essay on 'Development': it seemed to him to open the way to destructively novel theories, and did not obviously consort with the views of Pusey and Keble on 'the faith once delivered,' and the rule of what was 'always, everywhere, by all' accepted for true. The weakness of the Tractarian appeal to antiquity was always its extremely static character.

Still, Pusey determined to maintain his attitude of friendly neutrality towards Rome. His researches into the ancient Fathers taught him that on certain controverted points the Church of Rome was at least as nearly right as the Church of England. The ancient Church did teach a doctrine of purification after death, and did in some manner invoke the prayers of the saints. The two chief causes which, as he saw, were leading Anglicans into secession, were the uncertainty with which the official voice of the Church of England bore testimony to the faith, and the desire, to which the Church of England failed to show a proper sympathy, for manifesting in outward form the spiritual unity of Christians. He allowed that Rome winked at popular exaggerations of the belief in purgatory and the practice of invocation; but her actual formularies were guarded and restrained. He admitted the hardness of the Roman doctrine of unity, and the rigorism and self-confidence with which it was enforced; yet Rome did know her own mind, and did care for unity; and no one could minimize the feebleness of Anglican leadership. Faults were not all on one side. He meant to bear his witness by living and dying in the Church of England, but he would not lead an Anglican assault into the breaches of the Roman wall.

The result of the legal action on *Essays and Reviews* in 1864 was variously received by Roman Catholics. Pusey summarized their attitude as follows. "While I know that a very earnest body of Roman Catholics rejoice in all the workings of God the Holy Ghost in the Church of England (whatever they think of her), and are saddened in what weakens her who is, in God's hands, the great bulwark against infidelity in this land, others seemed to be in an ecstasy of triumph at this victory of Satan." This was tremendously strong language for the gentle Pusey to employ, and Manning, at whom many thought the comment to be aimed, replied in a pamphlet which, while not wholly unconciliatory, treated the Church of his baptism with uncompromising severity. Pusey's answer was twofold: he republished *Tract 90* with a historical preface, by way of reasserting the claim that the Articles, literally and grammatically examined, were compatible with the Catholic faith; and he issued his first *Eirenicon*. In this work he vindicated the Catholic character of the Church of England against Manning (who became Archbishop of Westminster in 1865, while the *Eirenicon* was in preparation); criticized certain elements of popular Roman teaching; invited Rome to meet Anglican difficulties by an acknowledgment that the popular exaggerations which went beyond her formal statements of doctrine were no necessary part of the faith; and reaffirmed the signs that the Holy Ghost was organically working, not merely in the souls of individual members of the English Church, but also in and through her whole constitution as a spiritual society.

It was promptly argued that Pusey was accepting the whole cycle of Roman doctrine, as Ward had boasted that he did twenty years before. The demand was made in a newspaper that either Pusey should be stripped of his degrees, or Ward have his restored; Pusey confessed himself unable to decide which alternative was really desired by his critic. But in fact the two cases were entirely dissimilar. Ward had, in his Anglican no less than in his Roman days, an Ultramontane mind, and wished to establish the whole practical Roman system throughout Christendom. Pusey, on the other hand, had an irrefragably Anglican mind, and aimed at no smaller triumph than the profession of Anglican principles by Rome. If it seems the dream of an idiot to have cherished such a hope, since Rome was already practically committed to the view that the Pope is the necessary centre of unity and enjoys a universal jurisdiction—as Newman pointed out to Pusey—still the final seal had not as yet been put on that doctrine, and it was well known that strong historical and traditional objections would be raised in opposition tó any attempt to decree papal infallibility. Rome had gone far in the direction of making unity the test of truth instead of truth the test of unity, which was in substance the Tractarian position; but no formal dogmatic decision existed to prevent her from retracing her steps. If she could be persuaded to stand on a reasonable interpretation of the decrees of the Council of Trent, the Thirty-nine Articles really presented no insuperable barrier to agreement.

Accordingly Pusey spent a strenuous ten days of October 1865 interviewing the Archbishop of Paris and other French ecclesiastics, and commending to their considerate ears the principles of the *Eirenicon*. At Chartres he observed a number of little children being taught to kneel down and kiss "a handsomely-dressed Madonna with brilliant glass eyes." At Rouen he saw a whole range of tablets running the length of the church, and inscribed: 'I called upon Mary and she heard me.' Though this sort of devotion was exactly what created the greatest difficulties in his own mind about reunion, his letter (written to his ally, Bishop Forbes) makes no comment, since the Archbishop of Paris had proved moderate, far-sighted, and conciliatory. On his return he found a deluge of congratulation in his post-bag, approving of the *Eirenicon*: the wonder was increased by the inclusion of hearty thanks from two English Bishops. Döllinger also wrote: "I am convinced by reading your *Eirenicon* that inwardly we are united in our religious convictions, although externally we belong to two separated Churches"; coming from one of the two most learned historians in the Roman communion, this gave a good augury. The book was also favourably reviewed in a Romanist periodical. But most English Romanists were either lukewarm, like Newman, who was inclined to resent its criticisms of the popular Roman system, and complained that Pusey discharged his olive-branch from a catapult; or else actively and purposefully hostile, like Manning and Ward.

Time was short if an impression was to be made on the Roman authorities, as the convocation of a Roman Council was expected shortly; so December saw Pusey once more across the Channel, where he was received in the most friendly way by a number of prelates and theologians, among them Dupanloup, the famous Bishop of Orleans. One eminent theologian saluted him as a true brother; an archbishop introduced him to a somewhat startled subordinate as a fellow-Catholic. He was encouraged

to persevere with his efforts for reunion on the basis
of the Council of Trent, and told that the meaning of
papal supremacy had nowhere been defined, so that
no difficulty was to be apprehended on that score.
He came back full of comfort, to a scene of far more
deeply-marked divisions. Protestant activity in the
Church of England was gathering to a poisonous
head in opposition to the revival of Catholic ceremonial in parish churches which had come under
Tractarian influence; Manning and his friends were
moving heaven and Acheron to checkmate Pusey's
efforts; and Keble was struck down and parted by
death in the following spring. But Pusey continued
his customary labours, spending the leisure of 1867
in assisting the Bishop of Brechin to produce his
Explanation of the Thirty-nine Articles on the lines of
Tract 90. On the publication of this important work
the Bishop paid a disappointing visit to Rome, but
received an extremely candid letter from Döllinger
in which it was suggested that, while both sides had
something to disown, events were moving towards
reunion between Rome and Canterbury; the danger
lay in Ultramontane intentions to manipulate the
forthcoming Council.

Meanwhile, in June 1867, the Council had been
announced. Newman urged Pusey to organize an
address from a large and strong body of Anglicans
on the subject of reunion; the Archbishop of Paris
promised to procure a doctrinal decision at Rome on

a statement indicating the maximum Anglican con-
cessions, if Pusey would prepare one secretly without
Manning getting wind of it; and Dupanloup
volunteered to take such a statement to Rome in
person. What Pusey wanted was to be in a position
to say to the people of England: "On such terms the
division might be ended. You dread this and that;
but you see that all which you need accept, all
which is practically required of you, is to believe
that and that." But the scheme hung fire. On the
Roman side, he felt, the negotiations might be taken
as implying an intention on the part of a single
group of Anglicans to submit to the Church of
Rome as individuals if reasonable conditions were
offered. Nothing was further from Pusey's intention.
He was, and meant to remain, an Anglican; the
only object he had was to secure conditions on
which the whole Church of England could reason-
ably consent to be reunited to the Church of Rome.
Another difficulty in approaching the Roman
authorities lay in the practical necessity of employing French bishops as intermediaries. It would have
seemed more natural to the Roman mind that the
application for a hearing should come through the
Romanist bishops in England; but this was a manifest impossibility so long as Manning dominated the
English theatre of operations.

However, the whole problem was practically
settled in the summer of 1868 by the Pope's own

action. A summons was issued to the prelates of his own communion to attend the Council; an invitation was given to the Eastern bishops, who had been separated from Rome for eight centuries; but to 'all Protestants and non-Catholics'—including by implication the bishops of the Anglican communion— a general letter was addressed containing no invitation to the Council, but an exhortation to join the one and Roman fold. The status of the Anglican Church was apparently prejudged; Manning had opened successfully the biggest score of his amazing career.

Pusey next compiled, at great length and with immense learning, a second part of his *Eirenicon*, which set forth not only the belief of the ancient Church about the reverence due to the blessed Virgin, and its limitations, but also the teaching of the fifteenth-century Cardinal Juan Torquemada (Turrecremata)—uncle of the Inquisitor—against the doctrine of her immaculate conception. This was designed to show both the extent and the weight of Anglican difficulties about forms of devotion which played a great part in the modern Roman system, in contrast with the reticence of the Council of Trent. It appeared early in 1869. Throughout the same year further secret negotiations were being conducted by Pusey and Bishop Forbes, though without much hope of a practical issue, with a Belgian Jesuit, de Buck, who had been deeply impressed by the first *Eirenicon*, and tried his utmost to secure a hearing at Rome for the Anglican case. The Belgian was urgent that Bishop Forbes should attend the Council and claim admittance, or at least exert such influence as his presence in Rome might secure through the good offices of Dupanloup. Pusey saw the futility of pressing any individual claim, even by a Scottish bishop, and advised him strongly to stay away; the problem of reunion was not an individual but a communal question. Then Newman in September suggested to Pusey that he should go to Rome himself, since, not being a bishop, he would not be hampered by the embarrassment of any possible claim to membership of the Council. Newman realized by now that the question of papal infallibility would be uppermost, and hoped that Pusey's presence might exercise some restraint on the Ultramontane party which was pressing for its definition.

But Pusey was too prudent to accede. Instead he completed a third part of his *Eirenicon*, in which he set out once again the practical difficulties on both sides, and examined at length the historical arguments about infallibility, making it clear that he spoke for no one but himself—indeed, since Keble's death he had stood alone—and claiming that his interest was not to educate an anti-Roman party but solely to effect unity by establishing the facts. Copies were addressed to Dupanloup and other sympathizers in Rome, where the Council was now actually in session; but the Infallibilist party there, which signally illustrated its desire for fair investigation by denying to its Romanist opponents the use of any printing press in Rome, effectively prevented the circulation of Pusey's appeal to facts by its oppressive control of the local police and post office; some copies of Pusey's book were never delivered to the addressees but returned with the wrappings torn and the word '*refusé*' inscribed on them. Pusey's own judgment on the proceedings of the Council, so far as they were reported to him, was that everything appeared to be directed by human policy or stayed by human fears; "the Council looks as unlike any assembly guided by God the Holy Ghost as one could well imagine." It was, in fact, under the surer guidance of Archbishop Manning and his Italian associates.

In July 1870 the long struggle ended. The decree of papal infallibility was adopted by the Council. The logical conclusion of existing practical tendencies in the Roman communion was sealed with stringent formal approval. Papal promulgation was substituted for the consent of antiquity. Submission to the Pope was acknowledged as the fundamental basis of membership in the Christian Church. Dogmatic theory triumphed, as Manning had wished, over the heresies of history, and facts, as a punishment for their inconvenience, were made as though they had not been. "Before the Council," Pusey wrote to Newman, "I wondered whether I might not live to see the union of the Churches— I have done what I could, and now have done with controversy and Eirenica." Later reissues of the third *Eirenicon*, which had previously been entitled *Is Healthful Reunion Possible?* now bore the legend: *Healthful Reunion, as conceived possible before the Vatican Council*. Ten years afterwards Pusey said: "The majority of the Vatican Council crushed me: I have not touched any book of Roman controversy since." Döllinger had been sacrificed to a dogma which contradicted history. "All other questions sink into nothing before this. Our creeds must be reformed: 'I believe in the Pope,' instead of 'I believe in the Holy Catholic Church.' I have no heart left." Only one form of witness was left him, to which he had referred with confident reliance in connexion with the Protestant attacks in 1850—"death in the bosom of the Church of England."

Chapter X

THE REVOLT OF THE CATHOLIC LAITY

PUSEY WAS NOW AN OLD and venerated figure, but partly through his unsocial habits, partly through the independence of mind which he never forsook, he was more than ever isolated. The followers of the old Tractarian movement had separated into two broad divisions. An academic wing was represented in the universities and had won a footing in cathedral chapters; its members were more concerned with the theology and history of the Catholic religion than with its presentation in particular forms of worship; they were intensely devout, but uninterested in ceremonial matters, and were mostly content with a dignified rendering of the traditional cathedral psalmody, without imitating either mediæval or Roman methods of expressing the sacramental truths of the Christian faith. Outside Oxford, their typical leader was Church, who was made Dean of St. Paul's in 1871. At Oxford, not only were they represented by the majority of the theological professors, but in the third generation of the movement a much younger school of Liberal Catholics was growing up, formed of such men as Scott Holland and Francis Paget and the first Warden of Keble, who were afterwards destined, under the leadership of Charles Gore, to establish those terms between revelation and Biblical criticism which Pusey in his young days had failed to ratify.

The other wing of the Anglo-Catholic movement was popular and found its home in the parishes, particularly in those slum parishes which the Tractarians had done so much either to found or to revive. The laity of such parishes was not particularly interested in theological exactitudes. The people accepted what they were taught, with a better capacity for understanding the prayers and rubrics of the Prayer Book than was at the command of the Judicial Committee of the Privy Council; and then demanded that the teaching should be set forth manifestly before their eyes in form and act appropriate to the spoken word. They claimed that the rites of the Church should be presented with the full Catholic ceremonial, which, traditional in the Roman communion, had died out in England; hence by an ignorant misuse of language they were called Ritualists. In particular they insisted that the more elaborate accessories of outward piety should be devoted to the celebration of Holy Communion, which they had learned to recognize as the principal act of Christian worship. Already in 1863 a tract was circulating in some of the London churches in which that service was plainly called the 'Mass' as it had been in mediæval England and in the first Prayer Book of the English

Reformation. It was habitually so described ten years later at St. Mary Magdalene's, Munster Square. This development proceeded essentially from the laity, though it must be remembered that the younger clergy are necessarily recruited from that source.

Societies predominantly composed of Anglo-Catholic laymen, and founded for mutual support and protection, had begun to spring up in the 'forties. They received a strong impulse from the Gorham judgment and the riots raised by Protestant rowdies at St. George's-in-the-East in 1859. In 1860 eleven such societies in all parts of the country combined to form the English Church Union. Keble was an original member; Pusey, with his habitual caution, stood aloof. Numerous guilds, formed rather for the encouragement of devotion than for actual protection, also exercised no little influence on lay enthusiasm. Another factor of great importance was the establishment in 1863 of *The Church Times*, a weekly newspaper uncompromisingly devoted to the furtherance of the Catholic cause. Though the most distinguished member of the staff was Dr. Littledale, a learned and gifted priest, its most vitriolic paragraphs were penned by a layman, who cared no more for the persons of prelates than might the Miller of Dee; and it was the laity that swelled its circulation. *The Church Times* at that early period of its existence was extremely outspoken, extremely damaging to the feeble leadership of official Churchmen, and extremely encouraging to the aggressive spirit of the Church militant. In 1880 it was selling about twenty thousand copies weekly, but its sympathetic readers numbered far more than the total of the copies sold.

Pusey was not included in that class. He hated everything which savoured of ridicule or sarcasm, or which tended to promote disobedience to authority. "When I have read *The Church Times*, the correspondence of the clergy has pained me more than the editor's articles which pained me." "A wide evil is not to be corrected, I think, by individual priests disobeying their bishops." He was also profoundly suspicious of the Ritualist movement. People's minds were being taken off the glorious truths of religion, to be taught about things of less importance—at the worst 'about birettas.' "Why should people say 'Mass' instead of 'the Holy Eucharist'?" The spread of ceremonial was like crowding sail with a storm imminent. "The Ultra-ritualists are risking the whole work of the last forty years." He saw clearly enough that the movement came from the laity, and that their demands were only the logical development of Tractarian teaching. But he was an old man, who had laboured all his life for unity. He was convinced—quite wrongly—that the popular movement could be controlled within the same limits as had satisfied its academic supporters; and that, if it were so controlled, its adversaries would be content. The immense strides which the Anglo-Catholic cause had taken towards official recognition, and the degree of acceptance which its theology had won, represented to him, by comparison with 1833, an overwhelming victory. He wanted no more strife. To consolidate the position already gained, and to preserve and extend the peace, he was personally ready to sacrifice any-thing save the truth itself. The only weapon he would use against compromising or hostile bishops was to pray for them.

The truth is that Pusey was much too sanguine about the prospects of co-operation—Tait, Arch-bishop of Canterbury since 1868, continued to main-tain an unremitting opposition—and shared to the full both the Caroline prejudice for non-resistance and the High Church disappreciation of the power of ceremony to impress doctrinal significance on simple minds. In the far-off days of the Tracts he had discussed the question of the Ornaments Rubric, and dismissed its claim to literal observance on two grounds. The first and more fundamental was that it did not befit the ministers of a Church in a condition of spiritual humiliation to wear rich vestments. The second and more practical was that the true interpretation of the rubric was disputed, and the matter must therefore be left to be decided by the bishops, who had, whenever consulted, pronounced against the use of the Eucharistic vestments. At a later day, though he wore them himself when he was celebrating in a church or convent where the use was customary, he did not adopt them for his private celebrations. In 1866 he could say: "It is well known that I never was a Ritualist, and that I never wrote a single word on ritual until a short time ago, when my opinion had been quoted against it." It was strangely ironical that the Ritualists were popularly known as 'Puseyites.' Pusey, who detested the notion of being a party leader, refused to write or utter the word. He said he was accused of 'P——ism,' or even of '——ism,' The last term, with its expressive blank, accurately denotes his personal part in the rise of the Ritualist movement.

But the laymen were right in holding that doctrine and ceremonies could not be separated. Their keenness for the restoration of long-disused ceremonial was due to their recognition that this was the simplest method of testifying, before God as well as man, to the doctrine which it symbolized; and Pusey himself had to confess that on the doctrinal issues he was wholly at one with them. With great firmness he upheld the principle to the English Church Union in 1867 that ceremonial should not be forced prematurely on unwilling communicants; the meeting was only with difficulty persuaded to assent. The only other way in which he was able to exercise restraint was by doing all he could to concentrate attention on the essential questions of doctrine rather than on ceremonial details. In the Bennett case he was successful in this aim. Mr. Bennett, the rector of Frome, was prosecuted by the Church Association in 1868 for his Eucharistic teaching. Pusey strove in vain to have himself included as defendant in the suit, since it was really his own teaching which was the object of attack. The Court of Arches acquitted Bennett in 1870, affirming that it was lawful to teach the 'objective, real, actual, and spiritual' presence of Our Lord in the Holy Eucharist. The prosecutors appealed to the Privy Council, but in 1872 that tribunal upheld the decision of the ecclesiastical court. After this reverse, the direct attack on doctrine had to be abandoned, and what Pusey feared came to pass; the conflict was diverted to practices which, while they represented doctrine, and could not easily be surrendered by those who had adopted them without seeming to surrender doctrine, were yet in themselves matters of slight importance. Controversy raged long and furiously over secondary questions of which the main principle had been put beyond legal dispute. There could only be one end in common sense, if not in legal determination; but meantime thousands were sickened by the dust and sweat of ecclesiastical passions, and alienated from religion altogether;

or, what was just as serious, were inured to the practice of valuing small things more highly than great.

However much Pusey mistrusted ceremonial advances and deplored the conduct of certain people who insisted on making them, his sense of chivalry brought him into the field; he never could desert a friend. His sympathy was engaged not only by the character of the organized campaign of prosecution which was now being undertaken against the Ritualists—between 1868 and 1880 the Church Association spent nearly £40,000 in prosecuting them—but also by the historical absurdity of many of the judgments delivered in the courts. The only way to challenge such decisions was to ignore them, in the hope that if the matter were brought into court again, a better decision might be secured. When it was pronounced illegal for the celebrant to face eastwards at the prayer of consecration, and bishops undertook to enforce this view, Pusey felt that it was time for himself to adopt that position. Other leaders went further. The two senior Canons of St. Paul's, of whom Liddon was one, wrote to the bishop that they proposed to continue consecrating in the eastward position as ordered in the rubric, and begged to have the privilege of being included in any prosecution which he might think fit to sanction. But the prosecutors left the dignitaries alone, and concentrated on harrying the less influential members of the rank and file.

During the Ritualist controversy Pusey started in strong disagreement with the movement, but was ultimately drawn by force of circumstances into its support. In another campaign his judgment was no less at fault, but his original attitude was more unyieldingly maintained. All his life he had contended for the truths of revelation, in Bible and creed, against the schools which sought to supersede, rather than to explain and illustrate them, by the conclusions of contemporary philosophical theory. In 1870 it was decided by Convocation to appoint a committee of scholars to revise the Authorized Version of the Bible. Pusey, full of suspicion of the cloven hoof of literary criticism, opposed the project and refused to join the committee. About the same time proposals were made to omit the so-called Athanasian Creed from the public services of the Church, and were energetically supported by many whose belief in the truth of every word of that confession was as absolute as Pusey's own. The objections made to its continued public recitation by those who so assented to its teaching were that its language was open to misconception by the ignorant, and that its theology was too technical to make it suitable for general use. Pusey's rejoinder was weighty. He truly observed that the Athanasian confession contained the only clear teaching about the Person of Christ which found a place in the formularies of worship, and claimed that its teaching was framed in the plain language of the people. Furthermore, in view of the sentimental Victorian delusion that people would continue to admire the character of Christ and strive to imitate his moral standards, irrespective of any faith that the human nature of their ideal was inseparably one with the creative Mind of the universe, Pusey attached the greatest importance to the warning declarations of the Athanasian Creed, as a necessary reminder that right conduct depends on right ideas. Up to that point, contemporary history has proved him right.

But he completely underestimated the force of the practical difficulties involved in the public use of the confession, and the motives of the orthodox supporters of its removal; and went to extreme lengths in his opposition. The question was not one of the truth of the formulary, but of its suitability to public recitation. Yet he and the faithful Liddon let it be known that if the proposals were carried they would resign their positions in the Church of England; meaning possibly to claim protection from the Scottish Episcopal Church. Whether they were right or wrong in their opposition, there was no occasion for them to employ a threat like that, which, if carried out, would have precipitated a disaster on the scale of that created by Newman's secession. The Ritualists were with them to the last man and the last biretta. The battle continued till 1873, when Convocation decided to retain the Athanasian Creed in use and unmutilated, while issuing a reasonable synodical declaration about the meaning of its warning clauses. As on some other historical occasions, the decision had been mainly procured by sheer intransigence, a method which brings inevitable Nemesis, even though the conclusion attained be the right one.

Yet another conflict, provoked by want of caution on the Anglo-Catholic side, and indicating beyond question that doctrine and not merely ceremony was at stake, broke out in the same year on the subject of the sacrament of absolution. The Church Association petitioned the two archbishops, who pronounced against confession altogether; and a particularly silly report was issued by an episcopal committee, which in effect stated that people who were perverse enough to make their confession could not be prevented, but strongly discouraged their being given absolution. It drew in reply a vigorous and temperate reaffirmation of the teaching of Anglican formularies, in the shape of a declaration signed by Pusey and over two dozen other selected priests, of whom almost all were parochial incumbents of the older Tractarian school of thought. Another similar storm in 1877 induced Pusey to publish, after ten years of delay, an adaptation to Anglican use of a manual for the guidance of confessors, written by the Abbé Gaume; he prefaced it with a long introduction on the practice of confession, and quoted testimonies to its value by a succession of Anglican divines ranging from Cranmer, Latimer, and Ridley to John Keble. The book was adversely criticised by a Low Church newspaper called *The Rock*. "In the *Rock* of Friday," wrote Liddon, "there is a long notice of the 'Advice for Confessors.' The *Rock* is angry, but disconcerted. . . . The providential purpose of the *Rock* seems to be to advertise good books by abusing them." There was substance in the gibe.

The Ritualist prosecutions dragged on, and Pusey, while anxious that some of the less important ceremonial should be dropped, was impelled to defend the victims of the persecution. He appealed in 1874 to the bishops to act as true leaders and Fathers in God to all their clergy, and prophesied that if they did so, as they had never yet done towards the Anglo-Catholics since 1833, all would come right. The answer was the Public Worship Regulation Act of the same year. Tait introduced a Bill to reform the legal procedure in the Church courts, strengthening the bishop's hands and allowing an appeal, which should be final, to the archbishop. The Protestant leader, Lord Shaftesbury, who was Pusey's cousin, carried amendments that ignored the diocesan court, introduced a lay instead of an ecclesiastical judge, and gave a right of appeal to the Privy Council. Rather than lose the Bill, Tait reluctantly acquiesced, and Disraeli rallied the House of Commons in support of the Bill to put down Ritualism and 'Mass in masquerade.'

The Public Worship Regulation Act began life damned, though not dead: as such, it was a fitting monument to the Church Association's policy. The clergy in Convocation would have none of it. The Ritualists scorned it, as an act of pure State aggression, spiritually null and void, binding no man's conscience. Pusey was worried. They ought to say what or whom they would obey. "Their line seems to me to be: 'We are certainly right, we shall obey our own consciences and what we think to be right, and shall obey no authority, spiritual or temporal, which contravenes this.'" He had joined the English Church Union on Keble's death, but when a resolution was now proposed declaring flatly that no sentence imposed by the new court should be recognized, he promptly sent in his resignation. Mr. Wood (afterwards Lord Halifax), the influential President of the Union, was most anxious to retain him, and the resolution was altered. Pusey's independence had won another victory. He continued his membership of the Union, and from that time till his death was accorded a virtual censorship of all its public proceedings. What Pusey and the Union did proclaim was that the secular power had no authority in purely spiritual matters, such as the suspension of a priest from the exercise of his ministry; that the new court, in so far as it was bound to frame its decisions by the judgments of the Privy Council, a secular tribunal, possessed no spiritual authority with respect to such decisions; and that in the matter of rites and ceremonies they submitted themselves to the duly constituted synods of the Church. The authority of legally constituted courts in temporal affairs was recognized.

In 1877 the final result was announced of the first case brought under the new Act. With an ingenious perversion of history, the court decided that when the Prayer Book said certain vestments were to be worn, it really intended them to be discarded. The judgment was by a majority. Among the minority were included Sir R. Phillimore, the foremost ecclesiastical lawyer of his time, and two civil judges: of these latter, one declared it to be a judgment not of law, but of policy, and the other termed it 'a flagitious judgment.' But these criticisms were made in private: the Lord Chancellor prevented the minority even from publishing their dissent officially. Such a decision, by such a court, presented in such a manner, made the whole procedure contemptible. Pusey's own title for it was 'Unlaw.' Dean Church's sense of fair play led him to protest sharply and offer to resign his deanery. But prosecutions flowed in. Many were vetoed by the bishops concerned.

Yet in the next ten years five priests were sent to gaol, for periods of imprisonment varying from a fortnight to nineteen months, because in their contumacy they disobeyed this sorry joke of justice. At the end of that time the Act was not merely damned but dead. Its chief effect had been to consolidate the whole Anglo-Catholic movement, and determine all its members to deny the spiritual authority of any court which tried to enforce the ecclesiastical judgments of the Privy Council. Even Pusey was constrained before his death to make public defence of the extreme Ritualists.

The course of the events outlined in this chapter gives rise to certain reflections that possess an abiding interest in the light of circumstances fifty years later in time. The reason why the Ritualists were irresistible was that the clergy were urged on by their congregations, and supported by the laity when trouble fell. The bishops were impotent because they set their own judgments of what was right above the law and history of the Church, and attempted the folly of justifying themselves by appealing to the secular power. State-appointed bishops may be devotedly loved, but are apt to be vehemently distrusted. Pusey relied on two active policies in order to defend his position—solemn protest and judicial enquiry. The protests were ignored, as they always will be ignored until bishops cease to act as a well-meaning autocracy and consent to act as a constitutional episcopate, subject and not monarch of the law and custom of the Church. In the efficacy of judicial enquiry Pusey put great trust. He detested lawlessness, and was convinced to the end that an unbiased court, if it might be had, could only decide in favour of the views he held. He attacked the Privy Council judgments primarily because they were unnatural rather than because they were secular. It was only when experience taught him that nothing could be expected of them, but what was unhistorical and unjudicial, that he fell back on the demand for a purely spiritual tribunal. He had a most profound faith in the power of law to arrive at truth and dispense justice.

There was more than a touch of legalism about him. If the law fairly condemned him, he was quite ready to bow to its authority, even though that would mean his exit from the Church of England. So late as 1877 he would not defend the revival of ceremonial which on a reasonable construction the Prayer Book did not positively require. When he had invoked the law against others, it was not because he disagreed with them—there were plenty such in the Church on whom he made no attack—but because he was persuaded that the law had already formally prejudged the issue and condemned the positions which they were adopting; the motive of his attack on the man was solely in order to defend the system. His stiffness of mind is curiously illustrated by his attitude towards the Old Catholics and the Eastern Orthodox. When conferences were being held at Bonn in 1874 and 1875 between Anglicans (including Liddon), Old Catholics, and Orientals, he was sharply and persistently critical of proposals to alter back the Western form of the Nicene Creed to its original wording in order to conciliate the Easterns; and that, although he firmly believed that both forms of words meant the same thing. Once the words had been accepted into the creed and become accustomed there, though only in one half of Christendom, he held that they could not be ejected without compromising the truth which they expressed. Towards the end of his life Pusey's sense of law became far stronger than his sense of expediency, owing in some measure to the indirect character of so many of his contacts with personalities, but probably still more to the posthumous influence of Keble. While Keble lived, his rigidity of outlook could be made the subject of argument and persuasion. When he was dead, it became sacrosanct in the pious memory of his surviving partner.

The Ritualists, on the other hand, had only desired to be tolerated, and had never sought to silence others. Their concern was not legal definition but parish ministry. Their co-operation with Pusey brought them into the way of uttering solemn protests and pronouncing solemn threats, a custom which unfortunately persisted, in regrettable conjunction with an inability to distinguish between vital and immaterial issues. A tradition was thus formed of fighting in the last ditch for the protection of mere outworks of religion, and the habit of meticulous protestation still hangs like a Pharisaic gaberdine about a small section of modern Anglo-Catholics. But apart from this, they were never legalists. Their experience of legal procedure gave them a wholesome distaste for it, mingled with contempt. The ecclesiastical courts are still unreformed, and still the Public Worship Regulation Act rots on the statute book like a hulk in a backwater: no Anglo-Catholic will respect a legal administration tainted with these defects. The consequence has been to intensify their tendency to private judgment, and to create a conflict of loyalties in their minds, to dispel which will require a greater insight and wisdom, and a more powerful leadership, than any which the Church of England has seen in the course of the last hundred years.

Chapter XI

JOURNEY'S END

FOR THE LAST FORTY YEARS of his life Pusey had
lived in his lodgings at Christ Church in great
simplicity, varied only by the change of scene and
relative relaxation of the pressure of work which
were entailed by such holidays as his health
necessitated. His health broke down entirely in
1864; again at the beginning of 1873, when he nearly
died at Genoa, after straining his chest by his exer-
tions to warn a child who was in danger of being
run over by a vehicle; again in 1878, when Newman
made his last conscientious effort to gather him into
the Roman fold; and yet once more in 1880. He
suffered severely from bronchitis, and, in consequence, lived almost entirely indoors, except when
he was staying at Ascot. When business took him
out, his slight but venerable figure was swathed with
almost as many wrappings as a mummy. About
1875 he became nearly stone deaf; penitents had
to write down their confessions. His voice grew too
husky to preach; his last sermons were read for him
by others. After 1877 he was forbidden by the doctor
to attend the daily Matins and Evensong in the
cathedral, though he continued according to his
custom to celebrate the Eucharist in his study, on a
marble altar slab which is still preserved and used in

the chapel of Pusey House. When he could no longer celebrate daily, he still did so on Sundays and holy days. His intellectual and pastoral labours never ceased.

The household at the professorial lodgings was a small one. Of his two surviving children, his daughter Mary was married in 1854. Thenceforward the crippled Philip was his sole regular companion and his constant solace. At his father's desire Philip devoted himself to patristic learning, searching the libraries of Europe and the near East for manu-scripts, and bringing to his edition of the works of St. Cyril profound scholarship and erudition. When Lady Emily died, shortly after Mary's wedding, her widowed husband would not leave his brother Edward's side. He was therefore brought to Christ Church, but was struck down by paralysis within a week. So for eight months, till he followed his wife to the grave, he also was an inmate of Pusey's house. His son was taken away from Pusey by the guardians appointed under an old will, as has been already related; but Pusey's nieces were permitted to come and stay with him from time to time, and they regarded him with the affection of daughters. He was never disturbed by their doings, but encouraged them to make music and to give parties in the house, over which some Christ Church lady was imported to preside. He had always had a special love for children, and was at pains, in the summer of 1881, to buy and forward to his grand-daughter a ticket for the Christ Church Commemoration Ball. He sat up to see her dressed for it, and at breakfast next morning asked if her partners had acquitted themselves to her satisfaction. Pusey was no Puritan towards the innocent.

His love for Newman was unabated, even though the main theological division between them was widened by the Vatican Council to an impassable gulf. After his recovery in 1873, he wrote to J.H.N., from Genoa: "All Easter blessings. I knew that your love would follow me at all times and under all circumstances. God reward you for it": he proceeded, as he often did, to consult Newman about some theological points. No barrier made by man could separate E.B.P. from communion with the heart of J.H.N. But other separations could not be avoided. The sudden death of Bishop Wilberforce in 1873 caused Pusey great grief; they had been strongly drawn together for a long time, and had recently fought as comrades in the theological trenches. In the same year he was reconciled with Hook, now Dean of Chichester. To his honour, the advances were made, through Liddon, by Hook himself. "Can you tell that saint whom England persecuted, our dearly beloved Pusey, that I should like, as I am passing out of this world, to be permitted to renew the friendship with him, which in my youthful days was my joy and crown of rejoicing?" Perhaps when Hook wrote: "Saint whom

England persecuted," he may have meant by 'England' primarily 'Hook,' as Nelson meant by England primarily Nelson in his signal to the fleet at Trafalgar. In any case, his gallantly characteristic overture was warmly welcomed. He died in 1875.

A more bitter loss was that of Bishop Forbes, who also died in 1875. Pusey had been intimate with him since he had been a curate at Oxford in 1846; for a short time he had been vicar of St. Saviour's, Leeds; after his elevation to the See of Brechin they had acted together on many occasions; and whenever he came to Oxford, Pusey's house was his home. An intimate legacy to Pusey from the bishop was a magnificent scarlet dressing-gown, arrayed in which the old man slowly passed from room to room on the arm of attendants. From 1878 Pusey's increasing frailty prevented him from scaling the staircase, and the dining-room, which had been converted into a large study, now suffered another change into a bedroom. Unquestionably, the bishop's dressing-gown was very useful to the old ascetic, who would not buy himself new clothes while other children of God were dressed in rags.

But the worst loss of all fell in January 1880. Philip went upstairs to bed in his usual health, had a fit of apoplexy, and was dead in five hours, at the age of forty-nine. Pusey was so overcome by the shock, and by the strain of watching at the bedside through the night, that his life was despaired of, and it was thought that one grave would cover both father and son. But he slowly recovered. In one way the sorrow which he felt was less acute than that occasioned by the death of his wife, or, in later years, by that of Keble; because he knew the separation could only be a short one. "At my age," he said, with a smile, "we cannot, you know, be very long without seeing each other again." So he went on quoting Philip's sayings, characteristically, in the present tense. It was not: "Philip used to say," but "Philip says." Philip's duties in the great empty house were assumed by James Brine, son of Pusey's daughter Mary, who was ordained in May 1880 to the priesthood which Philip had desired in vain.

The sympathy shown to Pusey on his son's death indicated the respect and honour in which Oxford now held him. The regard of his academic associates had, in fact, been well illustrated by an almost comic scene that took place two years earlier. The Dean of Christ Church called at Pusey's lodgings and presented an address, signed by every resident member of the Governing Body, imploring that he would consent to have his portrait painted for the College Hall, which contains far the finest gallery of portraits in Oxford. Pusey's extreme shrinking from conceit and self-assertion, and his dread of drawing personal attention to himself, had led him about the time of his wife's death to make a solemn declaration to Keble that he would never have his portrait painted. In spite of many entreaties, he had held to this determination ever since. Hearing unofficially of what was intended, Pusey wrote a long and grateful letter to the Dean before he made his call, declining the honour. Nevertheless, the Dean called. Every argument was exhausted, but Pusey stood adamant. He expressed his deep gratification at the loving wish, and greatly desired to comply with it. But he could not. "It is a matter of religion with me." So with mutual protestations of affection, which were in this case entirely sincere, the two parted. The portraits and bust of Pusey which exist, whether at Christ Church or at Pusey House, were executed, without his knowledge, either from memory or from his death-mask. In addition, there survive at least three published sketches—two kindly and sympathetic, drawn when he was about forty; the other, made towards the end of his life, a malicious caricature. It is curious that each artist reversed the current estimation in which his subject was held by the mass of those who were interested in him.

The same humility caused him to express a desire that no memorial should be made of him after his death. When Liddon proposed in 1879 to collect materials for writing his life, in order that the truth might be transmitted to posterity about the many controversies in which Pusey had been involved

during his lifelong struggle for English Churchmanship, the suggestion scared him. "People have made
too much of me, so that a little moderate abuse is a
relief to me. . . . If you thought of anything of the
kind, I should cut and run and hide myself in some
cave." Liddon retorted that if their side did not
publish a true version of events, the others would
give the world a version of another kind. So Pusey
consented to impart information for a history of the
Oxford Movement: "but the central figure should
be J.K." Liddon accepted all the information he
could get, and kept his own counsel. Saints—and
Newman had said in 1836 that there never was a
man in the world on whom there was more
temptation to bestow the name reserved for departed
servants of God than Pusey—cannot expect to have
their own way in everything.

A very good working test of saintliness may be
made by considering the degree in which devotion to
works of personal consecration is reproduced in the
form of devotion to one's fellow-men. Pusey stands
this test. He loved everybody, from the undergraduates whom from about 1864 he addressed with
touching sincerity as "my sons," to the nuns whom
with a like reality he called "my sisters." His last
theological controversy, that with Dr. Farrar in
1880 on the subject of the everlasting punishment of
the wicked who are finally impenitent, was dictated
by his conviction of the necessity of love to happiness.

Pusey easily refuted the belief that the majority of mankind are doomed to everlasting woe; such a faith was Calvinism, not Bible Christianity. But it must be possible for man finally to reject God, for real freewill implies the capacity to choose evil, and the more complete the freewill, the worse the disorder created by an evil choice; yet without real freewill there could be no real love. "Without freewill we could not freely love God: freedom is a condition of love." And to Pusey, as he said in an unpublished sermon: "The love of God, and the love of man for God, are one and the same virtue and grace."

But above all, if Christian love can be said to admit of degrees, Pusey loved the poor. This fact had struck an observer when Edward and Maria were on their honeymoon, and the young deacon, after preaching his first sermon, went round to all the cottages and made friends with the people of the village in which they were staying. He was deeply distressed by the Irish famine in 1847, and urged his elder brother, who was in Parliament, to be an instrument of good to God's poor. Reference has already been made to his concern for orphans and his interest in the economic employment of women. He poured out a stream of benefactions for Sisters to minister to the poor and churches to train them in Christian civilization. In 1866 he tells how his boyish mind had been impressed by the sight of a

poor man, fifty years before, listening with emotion
to the preaching of Bishop Heber in a West End
church, where, as a rule, the face of a poor man
was never seen. Simply because he was a poor man
among the well-to-do, Pusey had never forgotten
him. On another occasion he spoke of "our miles of
misery in our large towns." Country-bred himself,
he found infinite depression in contemplation of the
slums. Wretched social conditions were no new
thing, in town or country, but in place of concentrated degradation the industrial revolution had
created gross spreading pools of unending misery
round every great town, which oppressed Pusey's
spirit. The Church ought not, he said, to leave the
solution of social problems to individual effort, but
to attack them corporately. "We need clergy to
penetrate our mines, to emigrate with our emigrants,
to shift with our shifting population, to grapple with
our manufacturing system as the apostles did with
the slave system of the ancient world." Presumably
what he had in mind in the last reference was the
way in which St. Paul's love had transfigured the
relationship of master and man in his letter to
Philemon.

Pusey's own lot was not ordinarily cast in the
slums, but when occasion called he was ready to
face them. In the summer after Keble's death a
severe outbreak of cholera occurred in East London.
The old professor—he was sixty-six in the same

month—took a lodging in the East End for the Long Vacation and spent three months there, devoting every moment that he could spare from the library of the British Museum to the personal service of the sick. He said, with an allusion to one of his ancestors in the sixteenth century, who had been a Walloon refugee, that he was nursing his 'cousins in Spitalfields.' The Rector of Bethnal Green, who as Chairman of the Vestry was responsible for all the sanitary and medical provision, was at his wits' end to know how to deal with the situation, when one morning, as he was at breakfast, Dr. Pusey was announced with an introduction from the Bishop of London. Pusey was a complete stranger; but before breakfast was over it had been arranged that he should act as assistant curate and visit the sick in their plague-stricken homes, while Miss Sellon and the Devonport Sisters would at once contribute a large temporary hospital and staff it. With his peculiarly winning smile, gentle laughter, and exceptionally practical powers of organization, Pusey was a godsend. He even found a use for his academic gifts. The doctor in charge of the wards was unable to make some Jewish patients understand what was required of them. "I will go and speak Hebrew to them," said Pusey, "and then perhaps we shall succeed better." With him were his son Philip and his friend the Hon. C. L. Wood, of the English Church Union.

When, therefore, he instructed Sisters in the duties of their vocation, he was speaking of things which he knew at first hand. "See Christ in all, labour for Christ in all." "Poverty, which is the livery of Christ, which He glorified, which He endows with an almost sacramental virtue, will often have that which is squalid, revolting to the senses, forbidding. Yet what lies beneath? A soul, upon which God has, all its life long, been bestowing individual care." "Visit the poor with great tender reverence, as having borne trials which God saw perhaps to be too great for us, as shining perhaps with a radiance of divine lustre, the beauty of grace." "If we indeed love God, then we must love all whom God loves."

"The dear Doctor," said one in 1879, "is all sweetness and love." On his last birthday, in 1882, he wrote to a friend: "God bless you for all your love. Love is indeed a wonderful thing. . . . God says to you: 'Open thy mouth and I will fill it.' Only long. He does not want our words. . . . Oh! then, long and long and long, and God will fill thee. More love, more love, more love!"

Because he was all love, he hated selfish luxury. He once preached a dreadful sermon in answer to the question why did Dives lose his soul? "Why wert thou damned?" Not because he was a murderer or a seducer or a slanderer or a drunkard or an extortioner. "Damned, but not for any of these things which men call crimes or vices," but because "I had all my good things in my life and I had not mercy upon Lazarus." There follows a terribly plain description of Lord and Lady Dives in modern life, desiring the police to remove Lazarus to the workhouse in order that he should not spoil their appetite. "Was our Redeemer crowned with thorns, that we might be refined sensualists?" In the middle classes, said Pusey, who himself lived simply and slept hard and gave away profusely, luxuries had become comforts, and comforts had become necessities. And what of Lazarus?

Pusey habitually walked with head bent and eyes cast down on the ground. One day in Oxford Street something must have distracted him, and he raised his eyes, only to behold a woman's dress in a shop window, priced at £60. He was appalled, and referred to the event in the same sermon. "I could scarce believe my eyes. . . . Apart, as I said, from all trinketry, one Christian lady was to wear as one of her manifold exterior dresses, what would have removed the gnawings of hunger of some 7,000 members of Christ." And when the sermon came to be printed he added a footnote to justify his arith-metic: £60 would purchase 14,400 penny loaves, or half that number of real meals at a soup-kitchen. Respectability was all nonsense. "Those guinea subscriptions out of large incomes are mockery of God." To Dives it would be as well for a preacher to talk Chinese; no earthly language could be more unknown to Dives than the language of God the Holy Ghost.

And because he was all love, he also hated oppression. The last year of his life was saddened by the prolonged imprisonment of one of the Ritualist clergy, the Rev. S. F. Green, who lay "in a felon's gaol" at Lancaster for nineteen months. "It looks so selfish to talk quietly about Mr. Green's remaining in Lancaster Castle while one's self is in God's free air": he wished he could have been imprisoned himself instead. "Mr. Green must lie, deprived of the power of working directly for souls and for his Lord, unless he will own, in fact, that he did amiss in following a distinct direction of the Prayer Book, and giving to his people a service which they loved." In August 1882 he addressed a letter to *The Times*, enclosing a description of Green's discomforts and his wasted and gaunt appearance, written by one who had visited him in the gaol. Another correspondent retorted, making fun of the imprisoned priest, and retailing some flippant gossip about him. Pusey waited to ascertain that this was false, and then wrote a stern reply—the last words that Pusey addressed to the public. The gossip was "absolutely and entirely untrue. . . . Idle words," he continued, "have to be given account of at an unerring tribunal." This was written on 31st August, and *The Times* published it on the following day.

In the middle of the preceding June, Pusey had left Oxford for Ascot, as usual, accompanied by two or three large boxes of books. He seemed, in spite of a cough which had persisted for six months, to be in better spirits than he had shown since Philip's death; and he walked a great deal among the pines and heather. Up to his eighty-second birthday, on 22nd August, he worked much as he was accustomed. On the 24th he was caused some agitation, partly by the correspondence over Mr. Green, and had a seizure in the following night. After two days in bed he was about again; he received his letters, and wrote some replies; but when he tried to read his books he was too tired to attend to them, and his memory began to trouble him. On 4th September he had a further attack, and took to his bed again. His devoted friend, Dr. Acland, the Regius Professor of Medicine, who had once before gone out to Genoa to wait on him, was summoned from Devonshire. He immediately said that any one but Pusey would not live another twenty-four hours; but Pusey had survived so many extremes of sickness that anything might happen with him.

Pusey did rally twice, but from the 8th his strength visibly failed, and considerable periods of unconsciousness ensued. He knew his daughter, and enquired about his grandchildren, but owing to his deafness he was scarcely able to hear anything that was said, and when messages were written on paper he could not read them. However, on 13th September, when the doctor asked how he was, he answered with a smile that it was the doctor's business to tell him that. He recognized James Brine and Dr. King, and again on the following day he was glad to receive his younger brother, William Pusey. On the 15th again his mind wandered a great deal. He thought he was once more in church administering the sacraments. He kept on repeating the words: "The Body of Our Lord Jesus Christ, which was given for thee, preserve thy body and soul unto everlasting life." Someone knelt at his bedside. The old hand was promptly raised, and the husky voice said: "By His authority committed unto me, I absolve thee from all thy sins."

On 16th September his mind was clearer. In a previous illness his constant anxiety had been to know the time of day, so that he could, as far as possible, maintain his system of regular devotions. Now it was manifest, from words which he let fall, that he was repeating mentally the *Te Deum Laudamus*, the Prayer Book's most solemn hymn of praise. In the afternoon he sighed: "My God," and died. His Hebrew Bible lay still open on the table at the side of his bed.

INDEX

Acland, Dr., 173
Alexandra, Queen, 122
Anglicanism, 38
apostolical succession, 28, 33, 76
Arnold, Dr., 40, 48, 96
asceticism, 52ff, 125
Ascot, 120ff, 173
Athanasian Creed, 150ff

Barker, *see* Pusey, Maria
Bennett, Mr., 148
Benson, Fr., 114, 122f
Bethnal Green, 169
Bible, 27, 28–31, 46, 142f, 150
bishops, attitude and achievements of, 34, 57f, 66, 70f, 73, 75, 77f, 84, 85, 91, 105, 152, 153, 156
Brechin, Bp. of, *see* Forbes
Bright, Dr., 127
Brine, James, 164, 174
Byronism, 9

Caroline divines, 22, 35, 146
Catharine of Siena, St., 28
ceremonial, 63f, 76, 136, ch. X *passim*
Challoner, Bp., 79
Church, Dean, 35, 75, 142, 155
Church Association, 109, 148f, 152
Church Catechism, 3
Church Times, 144f
Coleridge, Mr. Justice, 91
'condemned sermon,' 72f
confession, 82, 125, 152f
Convocations, 91, 107, 150, 152, 154
Cowley Fathers, 114, 122f

de Buck, 138f
Denison, Archdeacon, 92
devotional manuals, translated, 124, 152f
Disraeli, 154
Döllinger, 130, 135, 136, 141
Dupanloup, 135, 137

ecclesiastical courts, 87–9, 92, 105–9, 148f, 153–7, 159
education, aim of, 97
English Church Union, 144, 147, 154f
Essays and Reviews, 105–7, 132
Evangelicals, 19, 27, 61, 129

Farrar, Dean, 166
Forbes, Bp., 92, 122, 136–9, 163
France visited, 7, 134f
Froude, Hurrell, 25f, 34, 64f, 68

German theology, 13, 18–20, 24, 52
Germany, 1, 13, 16
Gladstone, 91, 98, 127
Gorham, Mr., 87
Grafton, Bp., 122f
Greek Orthodox, 130, 158
Green, S. F., 172f

Hadleigh, 33, 36
Halifax Viscount, 122, 154, 169
Hampden, Dr., 37, 39, 105
Heber, Bp., 17, 168
High Church, the, 19, 34, 78, 89, 90, 146
Hook, Dr., 59, 84, 113, 162f
Howley, Abp., 39, 41, 70, 85
Hughes, Miss, 115, 118

Ignatius, Fr., 122
independence, Pusey's, 88, 90, 103f, 145–7, 154
intransigence, 152

Jelf, Dr., 7, 8, 11, 15, 47
Jerusalem bishopric, 70
Jowett, Dr., 103–5

Keble, 12, 21–3, 25, 32f, 82f, 110ff, 158, and *passim*
Keble College, 112, 126f
King, Bp., 127, 174

Laud, 42
legalism, 157–9
Liberal Catholicism, 142
Liberalism, 19, 28–31, 40, 46, 61, 73, 95f
Liddell, Dean, 164f
Liddon, 104, 109, 122, 127, 149, 151, 158, 162, 165f
Lloyd, Bp., 12f, 15f, 18, 23, 30
Luther, 29

Manning, 86, 90, 132f, 135–8, 140
Marriott, Charles, 83, 93, 130
Mozley, J. B., 127, cf. 49

Newman, 12, 23–6, 32–4, 63–8, 71–6, 110f, and *passim*
Newmanites, 25, 63, 68
Nightingale, Florence, 120

Old Catholics, 158
ordinands, 126
Oriental studies, 13f, 20, 35, 100

Palmer, Wm. (of Worcester), 34
parental discipline, 45
patristic studies, 27, 29, 41, 46, 86, 161
Phillimore, Sir R., 155
Phillpotts, Bp., 87f, 91, 118f
portraits of Pusey, 164f
Prayer Book, 26f, 33, 38, 143, 155, 172
Public Worship Regulation Act, 153–6, 159
P—ism, 147
Pusey, Lady Emily, 10, 93
        Lady Lucy, 2f, 50, 58, 93
        Lucy, 44, 56f, 114, 116
        Maria, 5–7, 14–6, 17f, 44f, 47–51

Pusey, Mary, 44, 161
        Philip, 3, 6, 7, 10, 93, 161
        Philip Edward, 44, 50, 55, 59, 161, 163f, 169
        William, 93, 174
Pusey House, Oxford, 160, 165

Real Presence, 72f, 92, 148
Roman Catholicism, 28, 37, 39, 66, 79f, 90, 115, 131f, 134, 140f
Rose, Mr., 18, 33

St. Saviour's, Leeds, 55–9, 84, 114
science and religion, 101–3
Scott, Sir Walter, 15
Sellon, Miss, 118–20, 122, 169
Shaftesbury, Lord, 153
Sikes, Dr., 41f
Sisterhoods, revival of, 116f, 170
social life and problems, 21, 49, 62, 113, 120f, 127, 167–71
Stanley, Dean, 96, 104
Switzerland visited, 9

Tait, Abp., 73, 85, 96, 105, 106, 146, 153f
Temple, Frederick, 105
Torquemada, Juan, 138
Tractarianism, 25, 77, 131, ch. III and V *passim*
Tract 90, 69, 75, 85, 132

University reform, 95–8, 126

Vatican Council, 136–41

Ward, W. G., 68f, 74f, 133, 135
Wesleyans, 129
Wilberforce, Bp., 53, 78, 91, 106, 162
        Robert, 86, 90
women, employment of, 120f